First Love, Last Dance

A Memoir

First Love, Last Dance

A Memoir

*Debbie,
Enjoy with all
my best wishes!
Nancy*

Nancy Rossman

To order additional copies of this book, contact:
Xlibris Corporation
1-888-795-4274
www.Xlibris.com
Orders@Xlibris.com
69174

Contents

Part I

Ohio, The Fifties

Each year, we anticipated Mom's long-distance birthday call from Peter, although none of us kids ever thought of it as more than a friendly greeting. Yet Dad took every opportunity to do what he did best—tease.

"Elise, it's after five o'clock. I don't think Pete's going to call this year." He looked around the dinner table at Richie, Sally, and me. "You know, he'll be your new dad if anything ever happens to me."

Then, as sure as the cows needed milking, the telephone rang. The year I turned eleven, Sally and I wrestled to answer the sole phone that hung on the kitchen wall. Dad and Richie rolled their eyes at the contest. Being five years older than my sister, I usually beat her to it.

"Hello?" I said.

A polite male voice drawled, "Is Elise there?"

Peter had a Southern accent, just like Mom and her family. He lived in Atlanta where Mom came from. As I handed the phone to her, I wondered what the mysterious old boyfriend looked like. All of my questions called for a comparison to Dad. Shorter? Smarter? More handsome? Could he run a farm? Mom never answered these questions or filled in any of the details. To us kids, Peter remained a shadowy mystery.

Everyone else continued with supper while I pushed fish sticks and cole-slaw around on my plate, watching Mom out of the corner of my eye. Her brown eyes widened and she laughed briefly, but she seemed anxious to end the phone call. Kind of like me riding the roller coaster at Chippewa Lake.

Dad never seemed jealous about the phone calls, which surprised me. If Peter still called, what did he want? Could Dad be worried and just not show it? I watched him eye Mom as she spoke on the phone, and I searched for subtle clues to his emotions, but his expression revealed nothing.

Mom hung up and sat down at her place, the one closest to the stove.

"So what did ole Pete have to say this year?" Dad chuckled. "Is he still sore about losing?"

"*Peter* is his real name," Mom said defensively. Her neck and face flushed, blending in with her short red hair. "Losing? Good night—after thirteen years, things change."

"Mommy, I hate these fish sticks. Can I have more French fries?" Sally butted in.

"If I have to eat them, so do you little sister," Richie said. "What did Pete lose anyhow?"

Dad put his fork down and glanced out the window, toward the silos. "He lost your mother's hand."

Richie stared wide-eyed at Mom. "You were going to marry *him* instead of Dad?"

Mom glared. "Rich, I don't think this is appropriate conversation to have with the kids. The past doesn't matter."

Dad ignored her and looked over at Richie. "She was engaged to him until I came along, but I swept her right off her feet and moved her to Ohio. Isn't that right, Elise?" He winked and resumed his dinner.

"Did you have a ring and everything?" I asked. Even at a young age, the material goods of a situation interested me.

She nodded. "I returned it, of course."

I struggled to imagine Mom younger, and with boyfriends. I saw her as Mother, even if my friends said I had the prettiest one amongst us all. They liked her red hair and Southern accent. Sometimes they pretended they didn't understand her so she'd have to repeat herself. Their curiosity and delight in my "exotic" mother contrasted sharply with the ignorance of some townspeople, who laughed out loud at how Mom said certain words.

"We have gingerbread and whipped cream for dessert tonight. Who's ready for a nice big helpin'?" she asked. "Nancy, I think *Mickey Mouse Club* is on."

"No dallying around afterwards," Dad said. "The cows and calves are hungry too." We dashed from the kitchen and crowded around the giant Magnavox that dominated the living room. When Pops, Mom's father, died in 1951, he left the television and the Nash sedan to her. He must have known just what we needed because no one remembered how we ever got along without both of those things.

"Who's the leader of the club . . ." blared from the television as we sang along. I pulled my mouse ears out of the nearby end table and sat proudly. Mom told me a thousand times I had to set an example because I was the oldest, so sometimes I let Richie or Sally wear the ears—but not usually.

"Annette is so cute, don't you think?" I said. "I wish I looked like her. Then maybe Cletus Garver would want me for a girlfriend instead of Marilyn."

Richie farted his retort. Sally held her nose and waved at the air.

The impish Sally with her freckles and wild hair, made everyone chuckle. She dressed her cat, Cinner T. Bucklebee, in doll clothes and pushed him in the doll carriage all over the farm. She hid books in the linen closet, under Mom and Dad's bed (where she sometimes took naps), and in many other unusual spots. She kept her favorite book, *Blueberries for Sal*, close at hand since she thought the book was about her. Never mind that she'd never had an incident with a bear. Sally loved tight quarters, frequently disappearing for hours at a time. Sometimes she took Cinner with her, which led to shredded linens or an accidental peeing. But Mom and Dad just laughed it off. As the youngest, she got away with things that Richie and I were spanked for. We tried not to complain about the preferential treatment—instead, we ditched her every chance we got.

The Spin and Marty segment of the program held our attention. Richie and I agreed that no one appreciated Marty. We debated what would happen next, but Sally, at age six, didn't join in. She concentrated on the opening and closing parts of the show where the Mouseketeers sang and said their names. During a commercial I overheard Mom say something about "kids." I moved to the back of the living room, closer to the kitchen in order to eavesdrop. In this manner, I had learned that Mom and Dad often discussed things about us after dinner if they thought we were absorbed in an activity. I listened for them to lower their voices as my clue to move closer. But I wasn't always the master sleuth I thought.

"Nancy?" Dad said as he rounded the corner and caught me crouched on the floor. "Were you listening to us?"

I hated getting caught, but I also knew from the teasing tone of Dad's voice that I was off the hook. He ranted only if we shirked our farm chores.

Dad had learned about chores as a boy when he visited Uncle Walter in Chagrin Falls, Ohio. The gentleman's farm out in the country didn't make money because his uncle worked in Cleveland during the week. Walter bought the ten-acre property to have room to "mess around" with a vegetable garden, a small barn, a few animals, and to enjoy the outdoors. Apparently,

Dad tromped around in the barn for hours watching the four chickens and two cows as if he expected them to talk.

"Wow, I'll bet you wish you could be here all day," Dad said to Uncle Walter. Uncle Walter laughed before he answered, "Not really."

Dad became a willing volunteer at the farm, often spending the whole weekend helping clean out the barn, weed the garden, or mow the lawn. And Uncle Walter liked the company because he didn't have children of his own. He found humor in Dad's antics and questions.

Dad's early love of the countryside and animals never wavered. After high school Dad announced he wanted to be a veterinarian. That news didn't sit well with Grandpa who wanted Dad to be an engineer, like he had chosen. "That's where there's a future," he said. Dad argued for a time but eventually relented. He went to Case Institute of Technology and got his engineering degree. He only worked for two years, however, before World War II broke out and he enlisted. Later when Mom met Dad, his degree and work experience in a highly regarded profession made an impression. "I thought his maturity and education would make him a good husband," she once told me.

As much as he shared his thoughts and ideas with Mom during their courtship, she said there was no indication that he thought about farming. Maybe the stress of learning to fly planes occupied his mind when they met, or maybe he hadn't realized that mechanical engineering at Republic Steel didn't interest him any more. Or, most likely, as a man in his twenties he hadn't yet identified what he really wanted out of life.

So, after the war ended, Mom and Dad returned to Cleveland and lived on the third floor of Dad's boyhood home in Cleveland Heights, a common situation due to housing shortages at the time. Grandma Lilly welcomed the newly married couple and their newborn. Lilly added levity to the household with her laughter, but a tense atmosphere lingered. Nothing pleased my somber and authoritarian grandfather. The few photos in my baby book of Grandpa holding me are the only ones in which he ever smiled. My father bore the brunt of all his criticism—Dad and Grandpa just never clicked.

Dad returned to his old job at Republic Steel and slogged through it until the union went on strike eight months later. He then shared his thoughts with Mom, and only Mom, about farming. She knew how miserable he had been, but she didn't know how to help him cope. Mostly, she tried to be a supportive listener.

When Dad announced to his parents he had obtained a manager's job at Franchester Farms, a corporate-owned dairy operation, it severed his relationship with Grandpa completely. Part of the package included on-site housing and that physical distance from Cleveland deepened the chasm. Only Lilly visited and supported Dad's career move. Shortly afterward, without amends, Grandpa died of a sudden heart attack at age fifty-six.

After five years' experience managing a farm, Dad used his veteran status to obtain an FHA loan and bought a farm near Lodi, Ohio. Even at six years old, I vaguely remember the confusion of move-in day. Lilly made meals while Mom put things away. Richie, then four, and I explored the dilapidated barn and out buildings while Sally, an infant, padded around in diapers.

"Your dad had tears that day," Mom told me. "But his energy buoyed us. He said to wait and see what he'd do with the place."

Old photos prove how sparse the farm was before Dad's many added improvements: the barns, a milking parlor, three fifty-foot silos, fenced corrals, and a remodeled house. Mom conjectured that Grandpa would have come around if he had seen how much his son used his engineering degree—an original do-it-yourselfer.

More than the building that went on, I saw a man of few words. He watched other people and listened when they spoke to him. He never hurried to reply and scratched his head before he talked. The list of projects grew faster than the completions. Mom must have worried about the workload he carried without much break or help.

I often caught Dad standing in quiet awe and staring out across the fields. Eventually I learned he defined beauty as a wind-swept wheat field, a newborn calf, the smell in the air after a spring rain, an American flag atop the flag pole on the Fourth of July, a mother ground-hog taking her babies for a walk in the apple orchard, or a deer in full run through the woods. He took in every day to the fullest, always seeing something new in nature that thrilled him. More than anything, he respected and loved the animals. It's possible they made him more comfortable than people.

An FHA loan, at a below-market rate, enabled us to have the farm but it came with scrutiny. The FHA administration set up a board whose members made periodic inspections to insure good farming practices were being used and that the business part of the operation succeeded. Through that board, Mom and Dad met Harlan. Even though all of the board members were farmers too, Dad resented the idea of someone looking over his shoulder. The whole notion that someone thought he might not be successful irritated him. He called them "the watchdogs." As he and Harlan got acquainted, though, Dad softened his negative feelings and even joked about it. Harlan's reserved and quiet manner on official visits to our farm probably made Dad change his mind. Plus, he won Dad over with ideas on ways to save money. Harlan knew the best feed stores, the best veterinarian, and he recommended Dad join a farmer's association called the Grange, in order to get discounts on insurance and equipment. "He laughs when I tease him. Only a real man is like that," Dad said.

* * *

Richie and I had big jobs to do twice each day: throw down the silage, straw the barn, and feed the cows. Even Sally had tasks once she turned six: she fed the cats, dogs, and baby calves. But we had fun, too. After Dad added a loft in the pole barn, we sectioned off a small area for a basketball hoop, and Richie and I played "horse" every chance we got. We rushed through our nightly chores in order to have more basketball time.

On one such night, I decided to skip feeding the last four calves. I reasoned that I'd be feeding them again in the morning, so what harm was one missed meal? Later that night, Dad arrived at my bedroom door as I busied myself with fifth-grade homework. He stood in the doorway with his arms raised, covering the top of the door-jamb and leaned in.

"Nancy, get dressed for the barn. I'll wait for you downstairs."

I hated to hear his firm voice with clipped words in short sentences. It didn't happen often, but it meant trouble.

"What, Dad? What'd I do?"

He glared at me. When I reached the kitchen, I tried to enlist Mom's help. She only nodded to follow Dad.

Once outside, I took three steps to every one of his. He refused to talk. When we got to the calf barn, Dad pushed through the gate without holding it for me. Bellows, low and wanting, filled the air.

"Uh-oh," I muttered.

Dad got to the pen first and stood with his hands on his hips until I caught up. The calves probably knew they had an audience and turned up the volume.

"What do you know about this?" Dad said as he knelt down so his eyes met mine.

"They sound hungry. Maybe I forgot to feed them?" I said meekly.

"Maybe you forgot?" he sighed. I felt the weight of his disappointment. I wanted to cry, but I knew that wouldn't work. He hated tears. I hurried to gather up flakes of hay and grain.

At last he spoke. "These calves depend on you, Nancy. Every day. It's not your decision to skip chores, understand? How would you like it if your mother decided you didn't need dinner?"

I cleared my throat. "I wouldn't. Unless she made liver and onions." I stalled and finally peeked up at him. He answered with a half smile, despite his attempt to maintain a scowl.

*   *   *

During my childhood in the 1950's, most farmer's wives worked on the farm. But no other farmer had a wife from a wealthy Southern background. Our Mom stayed busy in the house. Though she learned how to can and freeze, she closed the windows that faced toward the barnyard, and instead she concentrated on painting walls and decorating, making dresses for Sally and me, and ironing *everything*. On rare occasions I caught her sipping Sanka while she watched Arthur Godfrey on TV. I suspected that she didn't like the farm much, even though I never heard the slightest complaint. She loved to be on the go, even if it was only Lodi, Ohio, where an unimpressive square held a defunct fountain and a sad gazebo. Stores lined the square: Underwood's grocery, Woolworth's, Lance Electric, Benton's Variety, Phillips drugstore, Isley's ice cream, two banks, a Ford dealership, two greasy-spoon restaurants, and the Idol theater, which the owner proudly pointed out was Lodi spelled backwards.

Mom browsed through the stores and talked to shop owners. She learned their names, which she always remembered, and enjoyed talking with them. I once pointed out to Mom how one clerk had snickered to another about Mom's accent just as we left. It made me mad.

"Never mind about her," she said. "People come around if you let them get to know you."

She entertained herself in almost any store. But the browsing wore thin with me—and my usual question, "What are we looking for?" wore her out. She explained that shopping didn't mean *buying*, it was about education. I'm sure she considered it a way to socialize, given the remoteness of the farm. Other than Dad and his relatives, she had no other adults to talk with. Dad often teased her about how she could start a conversation with a person of any age. Richie and I were more in Dad's camp—quiet unless we knew the person and, even then, slow to make friends. If we had time to travel ten miles farther, we went to Medina. In comparison to our nearby Lodi, it seemed like a city. The square looked huge to us, with its towering elms and a multi-tiered fountain stocked with goldfish. In the summer, band concerts and ice cream socials happened every Friday night.

There were "real" restaurants, banks with ornate facades, large grocery stores, several modern clothing and shoe stores, furniture stores, professional office buildings, a library, the biggest feed store in the county, a hardware and lumber store, and a Dog 'N Suds drive-in root beer stand. Medina was heaven. Sometimes Mom drove through the newer neighborhoods just to look at the houses. She'd sigh, "Some day. Maybe."

Once in a while, Mom wandered into the barn to help with an extra-big job. It shocked us, but Dad always found some way for her to participate.

On one memorable day, Mom donned boots and arrived at the barn to help herd cows for branding.

Earlier that day, at breakfast, Dad had complained about how hard the job would be, but he didn't outright ask Mom to help. When she appeared, he smiled broadly and explained each person's job. Mom hadn't spent enough time with Holsteins to know they were nothing to be afraid of. They might try to charge you, but they always backed down if you yelled and waved your arms. Each of us had an escape route to block as Dad had planned to separate cows from the herd, one at a time, and drive them toward the branding pen. The first young cow balked and looked for a way out. I stood my ground, Richie stood his, and the cow headed for Mom. She yelled, but the cow kept coming. The cow picked up speed. Mom turned, but her boots remained stuck in the manure. She twisted and pulled out of them in her stocking feet and headed for the fence, screaming all the way. We laughed hard. Once she climbed to safety on the fence, she frowned. "It's not funny. That cow wanted to trample me."

We started laughing all over. She never showed up in the barn again.

Nevertheless, our laughter and teasing did not deter her concern for us. In the summertime, she showed up in the fields with Kool-Aid, iced water, or Popsicles.

On one sweltering day, a local teenager didn't show up for work, and Dad couldn't figure out what to do. The hay had dried to perfection and a thunderstorm brewed in the distance. He paced and swore under his breath like he thought we couldn't hear him. Richie and I stayed back.

"Say, El. I have a problem since Clifford didn't show up today." He stared off, maybe hoping she'd ask how she could help. That was how it usually went—he always waited for her to take the bait.

She touched his arm. "Is there something I could do?"

Dad paused a little. "I'd like you to drive the baler. I'll be on the wagon behind you."

Mom eyed the baler like a green-eyed monster. "Can't Richie do it? I've hardly driven the tractor, let alone that big piece of machinery."

Dad explained that Richie needed to drive the wagons to and from the barn, where he and I unloaded them before returning them to the field. Mom hesitated but finally agreed. Dad went through a lengthy instruction on steering the baler onto the windrowed hay and demonstrated the hand signals that he used from the wagon to indicate "slow down," "stop," or which windrow to take next. The deafening noise from the baler made it impossible to talk. Richie and I glanced at each other and smirked.

"There's a clanking sound somewhere on the feeder I haven't been able to fix permanently. If you hear anything strange, stop right away, because you'll notice it before I do," Dad said.

Things went well for several hours. Mom's fair skin turned pink in the harsh August heat, but she didn't complain. Time was critical. She paid attention to the driving, and Dad hooked the bales as they emerged from the baler and stacked them on the wagon. Mom admitted later that so many overbearing noises echoed from the baler that she couldn't pick out a rhythmic chug from a clang, but she assured Dad she understood his warning. She wanted to get the job done. She watched the baler intently, hoping she'd be able to see any strange noise. Nothing seemed out of the ordinary, and the job continued.

Suddenly a metal-against-metal crunching sound and a heavy oil and gasoline smell filled the air. A huge bang and smoke billowed out of the baler just as Richie and I approached from the opposite direction with an empty wagon. Dad jumped down off the wagon, red-faced, and wild with anger.

"God damn it, Elise! Shit . . . I told you to stop if you heard anything strange. God damn it," he threw his gloves and hook on the ground. Mom froze on the tractor with her mouth open for several seconds. She turned the motor off and climbed down. Dad scowled and continued, "Couldn't you hear that?"

Mom turned her back on him and headed the half-mile back to the house. Dad kicked at the dirt and yelled, "Where are you going?"

She pumped her arms and walked with purpose, never turning back. She almost ran. Dad jogged to catch her. Richie and I followed without a single utterance. Dad caught up to her and reached for her arm. "Elise, please. Come back. I'm sorry."

"No one has ever spoken to me that way. Ever. Who do you think you are? Find someone else to help you," she said and jerked his hand away.

The whole scene scared Richie and me. We never heard cross words between them. They hugged and kissed each other all the time. Mushy stuff.

We lagged behind Dad to the house and upstairs to their bedroom. She pulled out a suitcase from the closet and threw clothes in. Sally showed up with her cat and cried.

"Where's Mommy going?"

Dad ordered all of us downstairs and closed the door. We huddled at the bottom the stairs. We heard Mom start to cry. Muffled voices and distance kept us from understanding what they said. But, that day ended Mom's farm machinery driving experience.

My guess is that Dad's excuse might have been the heat, all the additional work of harvest season, or frustration over not having enough help. But apparently she quickly forgave him. I never heard an outburst like that from him again, and Mom cemented her role on the farm once and for all.

The months of July and August meant grinding wheat for grain, cutting the leftover stalks for straw, and preparing corn for silage. Dad finally learned he needed to hire several high school boys for daily manual labor. The hot summer days drained me. I complained to Mom and Dad that it didn't seem fair that Richie and I worked as hard as the high school boys but we only got our weekly allowance as pay. Mom agreed, while Dad said he'd think about it.

With her prodding, Dad decided to pay Richie and me a penny per bale as long as the wagons were unloaded. A counter on the baler made the whole process easy to calculate. By then, Richie and I took turns driving the baler, and the rest of the crew shuffled wagons to and from the barn, unloaded them and then headed back to the fields. The incentive wore everyone out. Richie and I constantly strived to break the existing record. If no machinery malfunctioned, we processed seven or eight hundred bales a day. Once, and only once, we handled over one thousand bales. That evening, after everyone left, Richie and I unloaded the last wagon in near darkness. Dad laughed and proclaimed an extra bonus of a trip to Dairy Queen with no price limit on our selections.

*   *   *

Mom and Dad met in Atlanta in March 1942. Through various church guilds, the Red Cross had approached area families about opening up their homes for Sunday noontime dinner to the navy men going through officer training at nearby Chamblee Field. Most of the men were Yankees and far away from home. Though Mom's parents, "Nana" and "Pops" Hunter didn't necessarily like Yankees, Nana wanted Mom to meet other men. For Nana, this meant any alternative to Peter Eaves, whom Mom had dated for almost two years. Nana never accepted him. She maintained that Peter wasn't *the one*.

"He'll never make you happy," was the explanation she offered for her disapproval. Nana tried to fix Mom up with all kinds of dates, which Mom politely declined. But when Mrs. Dutton from the Red Cross phoned about hosting a Sunday dinner for two navy men, Nana quickly agreed. Mom did not like the arrangement and told Nana how desperate it would look to the navy men.

"They'll think you're trying to find a husband for your daughter," Mom said. Nana waved it off and went ahead with her plans.

"We're only extending our Southern hospitality to these officers who defend and protect us," she insisted.

The day of the dinner Mom helped Nana prepare for the event. She wondered what the visitors would think of the family's tasteful home in the upscale Ansley Park neighborhood. She invited her friend Emma for support—and because there were to be two men. A splendid table was laid, set with Rosenthal china, linens, sterling silver, and a crystal bowl with floating gardenias as a centerpiece. Elaborate Sunday dinners with Claudie's famous chicken were the norm, often with friends or relatives invited to round out the oversized walnut table. Everyone respected Nana's ability to keep the temperamental cook a part of the Hunter household, considering she had moved around to several employers before staying put. In the fifteen years Claudie had worked for the Hunters, not even Nana learned the magic ingredient to the fried chicken.

Nana seemed excited about the dinner, her normally serious nature interrupted with giddy spells as she put the finishing touches on the table and stood back to inspect. Mom tried not to think of the whole ordeal as a "date." However, Dad said the minute Pops opened the door that day, he realized he had the opportunity of a lifetime. "I never saw a more beautiful woman," he told me.

Dad had appeal too, as a blond, blue-eyed man with a chiseled face. Mom recalled that she didn't know exactly what to expect, but she hadn't expected that. His beautiful smile and shyness appealed to her. Dad talked very little during the dinner, while his friend, John, rambled on and on. No one knew if John had more interest in trying to impress Emma or hearing himself talk.

Pops usual friendly nature and interest in others made conversation easy. And Nana, uncharacteristically, warmed to Dad immediately. Mom noticed right away.

"I thought Rich was handsome," she recalled, "but I wondered what Mother saw so quickly that I missed. It made me curious."

There may have been another reason for his initial appeal. When Dad talked, Mom remembered the only other Yankee she'd ever known, a boy in her sixth grade class named James. She had loved the way he spoke and developed a bit of a crush on him. The fascination lasted only a year since James and his family moved back to their home state of Pennsylvania. She thought Dad's accent sounded just like his had.

Pops asked John and Dad where they were from, and he enquired about their families, and the navy. Because Pops read the paper daily, he kept up on current events. He studied the newspaper like it was his job, which to some extent it was. As secretary-treasurer of Georgia Savings, he felt compelled to always be in the know in order to ensure the solvency of the bank—a lingering fear due to Depression-era bank failures.

When Pops asked specific questions about the transport planes, PBY's and PBM's that the men flew, Mom said he probed with great detail. She had no idea Pops knew so much about the airplanes. Dad beamed and replied with enthusiasm. All three men debated the efficiency of the U.S. military, how long the war would last, and the human toll. By the end of the discussion, Dad admitted how disappointed he was that things had developed as they had. "War is ugly, and makes strange bedfellows of us all. While my sister is working for the Red Cross, I am learning the other side of the equation," he said.

After that, Dad quieted. He told me he stole a long look at Mom every chance he got. "She laughed a lot and had an easy way about her," he repeated whenever I asked about that first afternoon.

When dinner ended, Mom and Emma took the men on a driving tour of Atlanta. Mom drove Pops' new Chevy through Buckhead, Georgia Tech, and the Eastlake Country Club. Dad hardly said three words, and Mom worried that the tour had bored him. Eventually, he loosened up and teased her about her driving in a funny way that she found charming.

The warm air, along with dogwoods in bloom and azalea buds dotting the landscape, created a true springtime atmosphere. "It was the perfect weather for romance," Mom told me as she reminisced and giggled. "Well, probably not so much for John and Emma."

At the end of the evening, Dad asked if he could call her. His request surprised her, but she liked him and quickly said yes. Even though she had an engagement ring she'd taken from Peter almost a year before, she found herself curious about Dad.

A week passed before Dad called. They planned an outing to the movie, *Top Hat* with Fred Astaire and Ginger Rogers. Mom had seen it once, but she wanted to go again. She never tired of watching dancers. Afterward they walked to Piedmont Park. When Mom asked him what he thought of the movie he said, "Wow. That was a lot of dancing." She laughed because she thought he meant it as a joke. He grabbed her hand and held it for the rest of the walk. It gave her goose bumps.

The balmy weather, Southern hospitality, gracious lifestyle, and attention from a beautiful redhead all contributed to Dad's enchantment with Georgia, even though he felt out of his element in every regard.

His Midwestern upbringing had involved education, hard work, reserve, and function. There had never been an emphasis on status, beauty, or fashion. And yet he seemed to appreciate these aspects of Southern culture. He never tired of asking Mom her opinion of things. "I'd never met a man more curious about how women thought. Until your Dad, I was accustomed to men who told me how things were or should be," Mom said.

Dad returned for another family dinner two days later. He brought Nana a book on Ohio landmarks. She immediately pored over it and asked questions. When Dad answered, she hung on every word.

After dinner, Mom and Dad retraced their steps to Piedmont Park. Dad fidgeted on the walk, like he had something on his mind but didn't know how to say it.

"What is wrong with your dad? His cheek looks badly depressed," he said.

Mom nodded, so accustomed to the radiation treatments and seeing Pops every day that she hadn't realized it had become so noticeable.

"Pops has cancer. They found it in his gums after he had a tooth removed. Right now he is going through a daily experimental radiation process at Emory University. We're hopeful they can cure him."

She started to cry. Dad put an arm around her. Mom explained that she dropped out of college because of Pops' condition. Someone needed to take him for the daily treatments, and Nana didn't drive.

They continued to walk, each in their own thoughts.

"Pops seems very positive. A fighter. I'm sure things will work out fine," Dad said.

Mom liked the encouragement. Until then she hadn't let on to anyone just how much the whole situation scared her. They crossed Peachtree Street and headed toward the marble-columned entrance to Piedmont Park. Dad pointed out a weeping willow tree at the far edge of the lake and told her how much that kind of tree seemed to be like him. "A little sad," he said. Mom wondered what he meant.

"Elise," he said softly, "I have to go to Pensacola tomorrow. And here we are, just getting to know each other. I wish I didn't have to go." She smiled.

He steered her toward the willow tree under the drooping branches. He pulled her to him. He kissed her long, like a man does when he knows what he wants.

"Rich," Mom said. "I'm sorry, but I need to tell you that I'm engaged." Dad grinned. "Really? Well, we'll just have to see about that."

*   *   *

The 126-acre Lodi farm might have been considered on the small side for success, so Dad leased another hundred acres from two neighbors in order to increase his for-profit production of corn and wheat. He always wanted more. A completed project only meant time for another. He dreamed of a better milking parlor, another barn, or better equipment. He often headed for the farm implement store to check out the newest items. The farmers who congregated around Brownie's store must have thought him odd: no farmer truck, no bib overalls, buying a farm instead of inheriting one, and choosing a life of physical labor when he had a college education. When they teased him about the latter he said matter-of-factly, "Think of all the money I save because I can repair my own machinery."

Brownie countered, "I can fix machinery, but I don't own a farm."

Dad grinned like he'd been caught. "I guess you're smarter than I am."

I wondered if everyone knew just how hard Dad worked. He never had a day off, much less a vacation. No wonder that he fell asleep in church, in front of the television, or out on the porch swing. "A ten-minute nap is all I need," he said when I'd ask him why he didn't go up to bed. All I knew was that no one ever had to tell me time for bed or to take a nap.

Richie and I believed that once Dad added all the improvements he planned for the farm, we could take a break. Many times, the two of us snuck into the house to play or watch TV. Mom always posed her standard question, "Are you two sure there isn't something you could do to help your dad?"

We never asked him such a question. Not unless prodded by her. He *always* had something for us to do. And if he ran out of jobs, he'd dream something up . . . like pulling weeds around the silo or cleaning out the storage shed.

My visits to Grandma Lilly in Cleveland offered respite from the endless farm chores. No one liked to visit Lilly as much as I did. Once every other month or so, I got my reward. In my early years, she resided in the three-story brick Tudor in Cleveland Heights, where I had also lived as an infant. I never tired of running up and down the stairs and playing in the sun-filled library. Lilly would pull down one of Dad's favorite books and read to me. When I turned eight, she moved into a cozy apartment in Shaker Heights. We walked to restaurants, Hough Bakery, and Halle's department store.

More importantly, I detected no animal smells—only the noise of the city. I'd open all the windows in the bedroom where I'd stay and drift happily to sleep at the sounds of sirens, screeching tires, and horns.

We got dressed up and rode downtown on the rapid transit and lunched at the Silver Grille in Higbee's department store. In those days, they had a special children's lunch with a miniature buffet and tiny china casserole dishes. While I enjoyed opening all the dishes, Lilly munched on her favorite entrée of Welsh Rarebit.

As a kid, Lilly looked to me like Mrs. Santa Claus. Within a few years I noticed the details: a rosy smooth complexion, large-framed body, sparkling blue eyes, a turned-up nose like mine, and thick snow-white hair. She laughed often. She liked games, especially canasta, gin rummy, and Chinese checkers. I don't think she ever let me win, but she might have. We baked cookies, planned a day at the circus, searched a toy store for a pair of play high heels, and she always gave me a dime to spend whenever the Good Humor ice cream truck showed up on her street.

Lilly kept a family photo album in a large wooden box under her bed. No matter how many times we opened it, a whiff of cedar always filled my nostrils. She would turn the pages with me and add to the stories I already knew. There was a picture of Dad as a young boy with Grandpa. They stood a foot or so apart; Grandpa frowned while Dad grinned, looking full of mischief.

"Was Grandpa mean?" I asked once.

She paused. "Strict is more like it."

"Did Dad get spanked like us?"

She patted my hand and tilted her head. "You have a much better father than your dad did."

On the page just after Mom and Dad's wedding pictures, I stopped to study a photo of them in a cornfield. Mom's long, wavy hair made her look as foreign to me as Dad in his navy uniform. They looked so young. "We were all at Uncle Walter's, just before the war was over," she said.

"Lilly, did Dad have a girlfriend before Mom?" I asked.

She nodded. "But, we always loved your mother the best."

I took a minute to absorb her answer before I asked the question I was most curious about. "Did you ever meet Peter?"

Lilly became flustered. "Oh my stars, the questions you ask."

I always hated going back to the farm after my visits with Lilly. Once when I returned, I told Mom that Dad had a girlfriend before her. I don't know why I did that, but she didn't seem surprised or offended. "I know, her name was Betty," she said.

Over time, Mom stopped questioning me about what Lilly and I did on my visits. She learned our routine by then and usually led with, "Was your lunch at the Silver Grille good?" or, "Did Lilly buy you something at Halle's?"

Once Mom said that she wished Richie and Sally liked the city as much as I did, since I had so much fun. But deep down she probably knew they liked to stay home and that I had the honor of being Lilly's favorite no matter how hard our grandmother tried not to show favoritism.

"Mom, don't you wish you lived in Cleveland?" I said.

She laughed, as I remember.

*   *   *

Mom and Dad never traveled to Cleveland, or anywhere else, without us kids. Even though we had extra chores on Saturday mornings, Dad always thought up a family activity for the weekend. We picnicked, explored Ohio state parks, swam, roller-skated, bowled, and went to the Dairy Queen. I only remember them going out to dinner by themselves a few times, perhaps an anniversary or birthday.

But on Sunday afternoons, Mom and Dad disappeared into their bedroom right after noon dinner. Richie's room was adjacent to theirs. When we played games in his room, or listened to his crystal radio, we'd hear them giggling or talking. I showed Richie how to hold a glass up to the wall, like they did on Three Stooges, and we heard their conversation, along with kissing. But we quickly tired of that lovey-dovey stuff. Sometimes we heard the bedsprings squeak. I thought all parents did that, and kids overheard such things.

Our family's other Sunday ritual was attending Chatham Methodist Church, where we became involved at Mom's insistence. Each week we either went to Sunday school with Mom, or the whole family attended the eleven o'clock church service. Dad, however, seemed to have many emergencies that developed on Sunday mornings. Sometimes I caught the tail end of quiet words between the two of them, if he had just explained why he'd be unable to go. Sometimes the emergency seemed to disappear and then we all went to church. But I preferred Sunday school. We had a teacher who made studying the Bible fun. He passed out jawbreakers if we answered questions correctly. Plus Norman Broadsword, a cute guy a year older than me, usually came. When we attended church as a family, Mom and Dad book-ended the three of us since we kids fidgeted and taunted each other. If Mom noticed Dad with his head down, nodding off, she'd nudge one of us, and indicate to pass it down.

One Sunday at church, Mom met Alta, a widow who had moved back home with her young son to her family's farm. Alta's infectious laugh drew us all to her. She saw the humor in everything. Her positive outlook formed a cornerstone of the friendship she would have with Mom.

The church had a vacation Bible school and also a theater group for adults. Mom insisted we kids attend the former, while she involved herself with the drama club. The year I was thirteen, Mom starred in a romantic comedy. Dad helped her memorize her lines, and we eagerly awaited her debut. Excitement filled the house the night of the play. Even Lilly came for the weekend in order to see it. As we pulled into the school auditorium parking lot, we were shocked at the number of cars. I was scared for Mom but she laughed and said something like, "Oh my, opening night in Ohio!"

It seemed odd to see adults I knew on the stage. Alvin Arnold, Alta's younger brother, had the lead opposite Mom. They did several scenes where funny things happened and the audience laughed. I didn't understand all of the lines where people laughed, but I pretended I did. At the end of the play Alvin kissed Mom on the lips. I gasped and stared at Dad. He didn't react, much like he seemed unmoved by the annual phone call from Peter. Dad stood and clapped like everyone else. I didn't like the kissing part, but I wondered if Mom did. Alvin looked a lot younger than she was. The whole thing just didn't seem right to me, but the incident didn't bother anyone else—not even when Alvin sent Mom flowers afterwards.

* * *

Dad's fervor for new projects intensified during my teen years. One Sunday when I was fifteen, Dad announced that we'd skip our usual picnic after church and go to Akron to watch the All American Soap Box Derby Championship. Dad patted Richie on the back, saying, "This might be something you'd want to do."

Mom eyed Dad, like she'd caught him in a lie. "*Who* wants to do it?"

He ignored the remark. It would be fun, something different, he said. Dad rattled off all kinds of facts about how the race worked and how the boys aged eleven to fifteen had to build their own cars using the same-sized wheels and axles. Sally, nine at the time, listened intently and asked if the place sold popcorn and Cokes. Accustomed to sneaking off with her books, she saw this as not much different from other outings. She gathered up a few of her favorites and headed toward the car.

When we arrived in the event parking lot, hordes of people, confusion, and noise overwhelmed us. The Medina County Fair was the closest thing to it that I'd ever seen. And even so, it couldn't compete with the chaos in front of us.

Over five hundred boys from all over the United States—division winners from all fifty states—raced in heats of three. The winner of each heat progressed to the next round. The ultimate prize of a trophy and a five thousand dollar college scholarship stayed on everyone's mind. Dad absorbed himself in the program and recorded the best time in each heat. Richie seemed to share his enthusiasm. After a bit, they disappeared to have a close-up inspection of the cars.

Mom sighed, "Oh dear. Poor Richie."

Two months later, Dad and Richie immersed themselves in building a car of their own. In addition to the construction, Richie stretched his young body every night. Dad said he had to be able to touch, and hold, his chest to his legs. He didn't want Richie's head sticking out much above the body of the car. "Too much drag," he said.

Dad designed the car and basically told Richie what to do. They set up their construction project above the milking parlor. As winter approached, Mom felt sorry for Richie. I overheard her tell Dad it was too cold up there. She was worried he might get sick. Just before Christmas, I helped Richie and Dad move everything into the dining room of the house which Mom had wallpapered a couple of years before.

Dad covered the dining room table with heavy, quilted pads like movers used. Next, he curtained off the dining room from the living room and kitchen with clear plastic sheets. Mom rolled up the carpet and covered the exposed wood floor with newspaper. The roughly hewn car sat on sawhorses on top of the table, ready for final detail. Every night for weeks, Dad and Richie ground away at it with a sander, leaving behind a thin blanket of sawdust. It got so bad that I wondered if the wallpaper would ever look the same, but Mom didn't seem concerned.

I helped Richie by keeping him company. I told him gossip from school and who I had a crush on. Sometimes I sang the latest hit record. He teased me, "You can't sing worth a lick . . . the Beach Boys would puke."

Richie's stretching got to the point where he couldn't bend over any farther, and he needed me to push him down. I loved to dare him that I could go lower. As I sat on the floor with my legs out and bent forward to lay my chest on my legs, he'd groan.

"That's not so hot," he said.

I missed my brother's companionship and wanted our childhood life of horse and other games back. We barely eked out time anymore for *Gunsmoke* or *Have Gun Will Travel*. Richie and I had been close pals since he entered first grade, crying his eyes out. As his big sister, and a third-grader, I knew my way around. I told him how much fun school was, but he didn't buy it. I took him by the hand, rode with him on the school bus, checked on him at recess and lunch. Slowly he accepted school life, but the shy boy liked being home. He much preferred the animals, television, and our fun.

We liked card games such as "war" and "concentration," and we played tag in tunnels that we built with hay bales. I told him stories, sometimes made up, which were his favorite. We did almost everything together, and covered for each other when necessary. When we were young, if trouble brewed and Dad couldn't get to the bottom of whom to blame, he spanked both of us. He bent us one at a time over his knee and slapped us with his hand three times. Afterward he'd explain that he wasn't angry with us, but with what we had done. Then we had to kiss him. For a time I got an extra swat for refusing to kiss him, but Richie showed me the error in my thinking, and I eventually fell in line.

From the earliest time, Sally did not like to be away from Mom's side, but Richie and I sought adventure. We roamed the woods, explored the haunted house down the road even though we weren't supposed to, and smoked cigarettes made from corn silk and newspaper out behind the barn. He and I formed a relationship that excluded Sally. Mom challenged Richie and me as the older children, but she sheltered Sally. Her different set of rules made me stubbornly independent. I rarely asked her advice.

As soap box derby fever grew, my sixteenth birthday loomed. I needed Richie's help. Dad said I had to be able to back up the manure spreader before I took my driver's license test. I didn't understand what that had to do with driving a car but Richie laughed. "He's seen you drive the tractor, Nance."

That truth hurt. Not only was I klutzy driving machinery, I was easily distracted with worry over tan lines and a million other things. I had a short attention span.

"If the soap box derby ever ends, I'll teach you," Richie said.

Commotion dominated the house the day before the big event. Mom and I made bologna sandwiches and Kool-Aid while Sally entertained us with soap box derby cheers. Dad and Richie both quieted, neither laughing nor joking like they had done during the months of construction. I asked Mom who she thought was more nervous. She said it would be a tough choice.

I searched everywhere for Richie that evening. He had hurried through chores and disappeared when I turned my back. Calling his name didn't help. Finally, I peeked in the shed where he and Dad stored the finished car.

"Didn't you hear me calling for you?" I asked. He stood by the car transfixed and rubbed the smooth surface.

He smiled in that shy way of his. "I'm scared Nance," he said as his eyes watered and his smile slipped away.

The dark blue car glistened in the twilight. Who knows how many coats of wax had been hand-rubbed over its surface. *Richie Wilson, Lodi, Ohio* printed in white letters jumped out from the dark background. I rubbed my hands together struggling to think of something to ease his state.

"Nobody is more ready than you—Dad saw to that," I said.

He sighed. "I don't want him to be disappointed in me."

I slapped his arm as if to say "don't be silly" and made one of my goofy faces to coax him out of his funk. But he remained stoic.

The next day, eight months of preparation and designing the car came to an end. It was time for the actual test. Lilly, Aunt Sis (Dad's sister) and her husband John, Uncle Walter, our farm neighbors, and some of Richie's friends showed up in Akron for race day. We congregated in the stands to cheer Richie on.

Two thousand or so screaming fans spilled out from the grandstand and up the steep 975-foot hill where the race started. People carried posters supporting their favorite contestants. Horns tooted, and balloons and flags flew in abundance.

There were 508 entrants on hand to vie for their respective county championships. These county champions would then race each other in a series of elimination heats with one overall victor advancing to compete in the All-American one month later.

Mom fell to her seat as she scanned the pages and pages of competitors. She seemed nervous as she searched for Richie's name. At last she announced he was in heat 39.

Following a brief parade and singing of "The Star-Spangled Banner," things got underway. Dad didn't say a word—but Lilly and Mom relaxed, chatting away and laughing about many things. In a little over an hour, the announcer blared out heat thirty-nine over the public address system. I saw Dad bend his head for a few seconds. "Is he praying, Mom?" I whispered.

"I hope so!" she said.

We all breathed a sigh of relief as Richie crossed the finish line ahead of the other two boys. I had never seen Mom and Dad jump for joy before. They hugged each other and everyone else around them.

Dad left the stands and ran up the hill to the starting area where the cars lined up before their turn to race. Richie told me later that Dad had yelled, "Good job, Son! But don't steer. Let the car drift a little if you need to."

Richie won Medina County and the next three heats in his division to advance to the finals. The last heat pitted Richie against the top two soap box cars in the state and determined who went to the All-American.

A boisterous crowd stood on its feet and yelled as the starting blocks opened automatically and released the cars for the final heat. A red car in the outside lane jumped out in front, followed by a white one in the middle, and Richie's blue car on the inside lane.

"Go Richie, go!" Sally screamed. I grabbed her hand and joined in.

"Oh my stars, oh my stars," Lilly said louder each time.

I couldn't hear myself scream. Dad leaped down from the stands and ran to the fence. The red car's lead increased. I offered up a prayer and Mom's eyes filled with tears. The 975-foot descent took less than a minute. In no time the cars whizzed by and crossed the finish line; the red car had maintained its lead to claim victory, followed the white car and then Richie in third place.

Dad stood with his hands in his pockets. He remained there for a bit. At last he turned to us and forced a smile.

"There's always next year," he said when he returned to our seats. No one spoke as we gathered up our things.

On the way home, Dad insisted that Richie ride in the front seat of our Ford with him. Every once in a while he reached over and patted his shoulder as if to say, "It's okay." Richie didn't say much, but he nodded as if acknowledging Dad's empathy.

When we got to the farm, Mom busied herself in the kitchen preparing dinner. Dad disappeared to the bookcase where he kept old textbooks, a set of encyclopedias, a dictionary, and airplane books. He pulled out a physics book and sat down in the living room to pore through it, searching for answers. Richie and I retreated to the barn for a game of horse.

Richie and I often spent hours together with neither of us talking. If a conversation started it was because of me. That evening, however, I had no clue what to say. Any dummy knew that Dad hated losing, but I wasn't sure how my little brother felt.

Suspense overtook me. "At least it's over," I said as I took the basketball from him for my turn.

He shook his head. "Only for now. You heard what Dad said."

A couple of Sundays later, Richie and I played gin rummy on his bottom bunk. Rain spit against the window. There wasn't much to do—fun or work—when such foul weather prevailed. Richie shuffled the cards, and I leaned against the wall. I overheard Mom and Dad talking. I ran to the kitchen and returned with a glass. Richie rolled his eyes. "I think you're too old for that," he said.

I shrugged and lined up my ear to the glass.

"El, I can't let him quit yet. We got so close," Dad said.

"Honey, he did fine. But he lost that last heat by a lot. The poor kid must have been relieved. Like a ton lifted from his shoulders," Mom said.

"He wanted to win," Dad insisted.

"If, and I mean *if* Richie wants to race again, it should be his idea," Mom said.

I dropped the glass on the bed. I told Richie what they said about him. At first he seemed happy, then not: "Dad won't let things happen like that."

Richie's prediction proved correct. Dad continued to study. Richie kept up his stretching exercises without a thread of objection, and the two discussed modifications to the car. Dad made phone calls to other fathers whose sons had participated in the race. The new information discouraged him. Apparently he discovered many allegations of cheating. A few cars had supposedly been filled with lead plugs, covered with wood-fill putty, then sanded and painted. (This made it impossible for a judge to detect.) With a combined weight limit for car and driver, Dad said that a lighter-weight driver and a heavier car would be an advantage.

After even more research, Dad decided to replace the car's wheels before the next competition. He bought several sets and tested them for speed. When the fastest four were determined, he used those.

Halfway through the year, Christmas gave us all a break from derby mania. Dad asked me to accompany him to Cleveland on a shopping expedition. I had no idea who we were buying for, or if he had particular gifts in mind. It was just fun, and indeed rare, to have him all to myself. He said we could have lunch wherever I wanted. Another treat.

On the way into the city I rambled on about everything at Cloverleaf High School. Dad had only been there once since it opened, and I believed—hoped—he must want to know how it was going for me. Many times I had tried to tell him all about the new high school, but he usually sighed and said something like, "Get to the point, Nancy."

Mom had a different attitude. She never seemed to tire of hearing about which boy or girl had done something strange, who liked whom and why, the results of the cafeteria boycott when they raised the price of lunch, or why the Lodi students got in trouble for refusing to ride the bus and instead walked the four miles to the high school. She remembered the names of all my friends, their parents, and special things about them.

Finally, I tired of my own voice and glanced out the window while Dad drove. "Richie said he'd help me learn to back up the manure spreader."

Dad nodded. I continued to stare at him.

"Well then, I guess if you can do it, you'll be ready to take that driver's test," he said.

"Yes. By the way, what are we shopping for today?"

He hesitated. Finally he said he wanted to get Richie a special bicycle for all the hard work on his soap box car. Plus, Sally really needed a bike too. After that, he said we'd have lunch and stop in Medina for Mom's present. Which meant I would shop for Mom's gift.

We finally located the bicycle shop on a side street in a dingy part of downtown Cleveland. The store sign hung crooked and faded. When the owner appeared, I noticed he needed a shave and shower. He looked Dad up and down and rolled up his sleeves. A large anchor tattoo caught my eye. Dad told him he wanted bikes for his fourteen-year-old son and an eleven-year-old girl. The owner studied me. "Big for eleven, ain't you?"

"Not me," I said too loudly. Dad poked me.

I busied myself in the front of the store while they headed to the rear. Soon, they returned with what Dad called three-speed, English racing bikes. The black one, Richie's, had a bigger frame and the smaller red one was for Sally. Bikes weren't my deal but I had to admit they were beautiful. Dad negotiated with the man a bit and we started to walk out before the man called us back and agreed with Dad's offer. Until then I thought you paid what the price tag said.

Dad held true to his word about lunch. I picked Bob's Big Boy, my favorite Mom had taken us to several times. I ordered for both of us in the blink of an eye, since Dad had never been there. As always, Bob's served too much food and I couldn't finish my meal. Dad ate his and finished mine—he hated to waste anything.

On the way to Medina Dad explained that he wanted to get Mom something nice. I told him how much she liked The Better Dress Shop, considering that she had taken me with her many times.

The store was near the town square. I tried to tell him exactly where, but he didn't get it. Finally, when I said "across from the feed store and next to the hardware," he nodded.

Dad parked in front of the store and gave me fifty dollars. The amount shocked me. "Make it special," he said as I got out of the car.

Shirley, one of the owners, greeted me. She remembered my name and asked where Mom was. I told her about my mission, and she immediately had ideas. I knew how often Mom searched through the rack of nightgowns but I didn't recall her ever buying one. Shirley pointed out several she liked, but I didn't agree. I liked the white one at the end of the rack: soft satin, edged with fancy lace and rows of ribbon. "What size is it?" I asked her. When Shirley said thirty-eight, I said it looked about right, even though I knew Mom wore a thirty-four. I reasoned the size couldn't be that much different, besides it looked like the perfect "special gift."

"White is normally for brides," Shirley said. "But I'm sure she'll like it."

I couldn't wait for Christmas that year. I knew the big secrets. And having that information was almost too much power for me. I wanted to tell Richie—he'd been so blue about all the work on the car. I teased him with the facts. "I know what you're getting. I do, I do."

He didn't want to know. But his curiosity got him, and he begged me to tell him. He had no knowledge of the shopping expedition so at first he wouldn't believe me. "It's really, really good. You'll like it. I helped pick it out."

That Christmas morning I couldn't decide which would be more exciting . . . Richie or Mom's expressions when they saw their gift. In keeping with family tradition, a sheet hung to hide the view into the living room.

"How come you still put that up?" I asked Mom. "We know who Santa is. It seems silly."

"It's tradition," she said. "Some day these memories will be precious to you. Just wait. Maybe you'll even do some of the same things with your children."

Once we were finally allowed to go into the living room, Richie smiled and patted the bike like a new puppy. "Thanks. Thanks, Dad. Thanks, Mom," he said over and over.

I hadn't even considered what my gift would be. I had been so preoccupied with helping Dad and taunting Rich with knowledge about his present that I didn't snoop. But right in front of me sat my special gift: a hi-fi record player.

When we all finished, Dad reached behind the sofa and pulled out the special box with the wide gold ribbon. "Elise, this is for you," he said.

She carefully undid the wrapping paper and then refolded it neatly. She opened the top and pulled back several sheets of tissue paper. "Oh my," she said and lifted the nightgown out of the box. She chuckled and stole a glance at Dad. He smiled and shrugged his shoulders. I didn't understand.

"Isn't it the most beautiful nightgown you've ever seen?" I said and moved over to have a second look.

Mom must have figured out, by then, that I had bought it for Dad to give her. "It's lovely, but it might be a bit too much for me."

"It looks like something a glamorous movie star would wear," I said.

"Well, you're such a good shopper. How about if you come with me and help me find something else in my size, and not so fancy?" Mom said as she hugged me.

*   *   *

Though my relationship with Mom strained at times through my teenage years, I always outright feared Nana. From my earliest memories, Nana looked old. She had no interest in physical activity, walked unsteadily, spoke firmly, wore dark rayon dresses, and spanked us if we were bad. Sometimes people remarked on Mom's resemblance to her, which I considered an insult. In actuality, they were so different it was hard to imagine they were even related. Unlike Mom, Nana seldom laughed. But whenever she did, it was at something so bizarre I couldn't comprehend the humor. Once when Nana visited, Mom piled all of us in the back seat of our Ford, and we drove to Cleveland to shop. Car sickness had always plagued me if I rode in the backseat. I tried to warn them I didn't feel well. Mom and Nana tried to keep me occupied, because if I got sick, Richie always followed.

"Hold on Nancy we're almost there," Mom said as I felt my stomach pitch. As soon as we pulled into a parking lot, Richie and I scrambled out of opposite doors and threw up. Nana burst out laughing. She laughed so hard, she cried.

As I remember, Nana took over the kitchen each summer when she visited. Mom didn't mind, and we all appreciated it because Nana had skill. Her rolls and biscuits were even better than Lilly's. Nana introduced us to grits, rice and gravy (instead of potatoes), green beans cooked slowly with ham for hours, fried corn, and peach cobbler. Dad said all the rich food made him gain weight, but he loved every minute of it. Now that I look back and think, it had to have been an act of love for Nana to trade her life with a cook and a maid in Atlanta for a trip to the farm in Ohio.

"Ma, this is the best thing I've ever tasted," Dad must have said a million times over the years. He was the only one who dared address her in such a casual manner, but she always smiled or giggled at his praise, then thanked him. We marveled at this stark contrast to her usual demeanor.

Every year before Nana came, Mom fussed about the house in preparation. Dad teased her that most of the projects got done just before Nana's yearly visit. I, too, noticed that the lawn and flowers looked extra nice then, the car got cleaned and waxed, and the house smelled of Lemon Pledge. We kids looked forward to Nana's visits, not for her fun but because she brought gifts of books, games or special candy. While she stayed with us, she also bought Coca-Colas and Popsicles whenever she shopped with Mom, she treated us to vanilla sodas at Phillips' drugstore, and she read Bible stories to us at night. But our relationship with Nana never had the warmth or familiarity we enjoyed with Grandma Lilly, who laughed all the time, played cards, loved golf and tennis, and made more kinds of chocolate candy than you found in a Whitman sampler.

We never talked about Mom's birthday calls from Peter in front of Nana. It had become so common and fun for us to see Mom squirm and fluster on her birthday that we almost looked forward to it. But by the time Nana visited in summer, Mom's February birthday was old news, so the subject never came up. Except one time, when Dad reminded Mom about her old flame in front of Nana. He said something about how a Yankee never gives up and poor Peter had no choice but to surrender once he knew who his competition was.

Mom flushed over raising the topic in front of her mother. She watched Nana listen, unsmiling. When Dad finished bragging, Nana looked him square in the eye and said, "He really loved her. I don't agree he surrendered."

Nana's words stunned both Mom and Dad. Nana turned on her heel and left the room without another mention of the remark. Ever.

I think Nana's visits usually lasted several weeks. Her strictness made it easier for us to say good-bye, which was quite different from Lilly, who we always wanted to stay. As the day approached when we'd take Nana to Wellington to catch the train back to Atlanta, Mom would begin looking sad. Nana remained stoic as they parted, but Mom cried every time.

Though she seemed anxious in anticipation of Nana's visits, Mom also missed her deeply. They talked by phone on special occasions, and Nana wrote weekly. I remember each one of the missives being four or five pages, double-sided. Mom saved a letter like a treat, until after a meal or the dishes were done. Then she would read it slowly like you'd savor a favorite dessert. Sometimes Mom let me read one of the letters because I asked so many questions about what Nana said. Nana detailed the trips Aunt Kitty (Mom's older sister) had taken, the visitors she'd received, boring details about the weather, and what each of my cousins was up to, along with their accomplishments. I found the information about my far-off relatives fascinating.

Nana connected me to my Southern heritage—a foreign world filled with a complicated etiquette and history. She shared stories about the Civil War and why she believed that most Negroes back then were not mistreated. "The war was about more than slavery," she said, although she never defended slave ownership. She read to us from *Uncle Tom's Cabin*, and she answered my endless questions. When I complained about trying to understand all the formalities of Southern culture she answered, "It's genteel." I'm sure that sent me to a dictionary.

Nana gave us a notion of coming from stock that was special. Hers was a sense of pride in forebears, not in wealth or possessions, but in education, breeding and accomplishment. She said no lady or gentleman ever used the word "nigger." (I had never heard any of my Northern or Southern relatives use it). "Negro" was a word of dignity and, according to Nana, no black person deserved less.

Mom didn't leave her upbringing at the Mason/Dixon line when she came to Ohio. Even on the farm, every Sunday she insisted we eat in the dining room with the Wedgwood china and sterling silver. "No elbows on the table, one arm in your lap," she would say. We waited for everyone to sit, took turns saying grace, and then passed food until everyone had a plate. Dad made us wait for Mom to take the first bite. The massive table, draped with a beautiful linen cloth must have reminded Mom of Sunday dinners in Atlanta.

When Mom redid the dining room with plantation-scene wallpaper, Dad really teased her. "Yeah, El, this farm is just like Tara." Nana made no remark the first time she saw it. I wondered whether she thought it was out of place in Ohio, but she never let on.

The only Southern relative to visit us in Ohio was Nana. Mom invited her older sister, Aunt Kitty, several times, but she never traveled north to see us. Kitty traveled to exotic places all over the world with her husband, Uncle Harllee, oversaw an extensive household, and raised four children of her own. Twelve years age difference and financial circumstances made it hard to connect. Mom fretted over the limit of their relationship. Clearly, she wished for more.

Aunt Kitty often said Mom grew up like an only child, since both she and brother Chase were nearly out of the house and on their own when Mom was a youngster. "Poor Leesie, Nana had a lot of influence," she said many times over the years. "If Nana didn't like someone, that was that. She never changed her mind."

As a child, I didn't grasp the significance of Kitty's words, for I had not yet heard the details of Mom's romance with Peter. All I knew was what I observed when Nana visited: how she directed Mom in which way to cook the roast, in what to wear, or about why I shouldn't be allowed to stay overnight at my friend's because they had an outhouse. "That girl's just too common," Nana exclaimed.

Nana also had ideas about social events and alcohol. As in, she didn't believe in alcohol consumption at all. Aunt Kitty told me recently that when Nana moved in with them in her old age, there was some trouble. Aunt Kitty and Uncle Harllee often entertained in their home, and cocktails were served at five o'clock, every day, with or without company. Each afternoon, Uncle Harllee invited Nana to join them. Each day Nana declined, until the day Uncle Harllee announced that Bobby Jones, the golfing legend, was coming for drinks.

"Oh my," she said. "I'll be right down."

Apparently, she so enjoyed herself that she never missed another five o'clock get-together. As the others imbibed, she sipped her Coca-cola.

*   *   *

When we were young, Mom piqued our curiosity about the South by showing us pictures of Atlanta . . . the house in Ansley Park, Aunt Kitty's house in Buckhead, and photos of our cousins. It was not until I was nine years old that we kids got to see this mythical place for ourselves. Mom's homesickness convinced Dad to let her drive the Ford Fairlane with the three of us kids for a summer vacation. I remember Lilly and Nana fretted over the decision, but Mom's confidence eased their worry. It was out of the question for Dad to go with us since someone had to tend the farm—or so he said.

The first day on the road took forever, and we were just into Kentucky. Mom must have been dead tired with all the driving and keeping three small kids amused, but we were excited. We'd never been farther from home than Cleveland. When we finally stopped the first night in Corbin, Kentucky, we shrieked with delight at the swimming pool. We'd hit the quaint motel and restaurant on many future trips south. The restaurant had the best fried chicken in the world and became the platform from which Colonel Sanders launched his chicken empire.

Once in Atlanta, Aunt Kitty's sprawling Georgian colonial sat on top of a hill amid three acres of pine trees, flowering shrubs, and formal gardens. It looked huge and fancy. The first time we wound up the driveway in our car with Mom honking all the way, Sally pressed her little face against the window.

"How many people live here?" she asked. Mom chuckled.

The trees were different than those in Ohio, and the air was thick with floral scents. Red dirt peeked through the grass and hillsides. There wasn't much to do, compared to the farm, except play with the intercom in the house, enjoy our cousin David's comic book collection, or slide down the steep hill over the pine needles in a cardboard box, much faster than a sled on snow.

Every morning, the maid Mat (Madeline) greeted us in the kitchen with hugs and kisses for "her babies." I liked to touch her velvet black skin, it was smoother than mine and glistened in the early light. Dressed in her starched uniform and white apron, she resembled a kid playing dress-up. She laughed at everything and cracked Juicy Fruit gum in her mouth. Sometimes, she gave us extra pieces from her pocket. We loved to be with her, and we basked in her special attention. Our first morning in Atlanta, she squeezed fresh orange juice and seated us in the dining room at a mahogany table that accommodated twelve. Crocheted place mats, crystal candelabra, and goblets with ice water were already on the table.

"We eat breakfast in here?" Richie said.

Mat laughed and disappeared, only to return with scrambled eggs, bacon, and piping-hot biscuits. For the rest of our visit, we ate all of our breakfasts in this manner, along with our youngest cousin, David. He had entertaining quirks in his personality much like Sally.

Mom had hoped Sally and David would become buddies—they were only a year apart in age—but that dream ended the day they played a game of croquet on the back lawn. David cheated, and Sally hit him over the head with her mallet.

For the next five or six summers, we continued the tradition of tripping south to spend a week with Mom's relatives. Once Aunt Kitty suggested we all go to their cabin in Lakemont, Georgia, on Lake Rabun. We swam all day, floated on inner tubes, water skied once we were taught, and drank frozen Cokes from a cooler on the back porch, just like one you'd see in at a gas station.

Large rustic cabins, boathouses, and docks dotted the densely tree-lined body of water. Lake Rabun, a man-made reservoir, had been created to generate power and thereby had an enormous dam at one end. With no restaurants, no nearby grocery, and only primitive phone service, it was tranquil and beautiful. Due to its shortcomings, no one lived there year-round. The single-lane, heavily rutted dirt road up to the cabin outdid anything we had on the farm. But once we arrived, a complete vacation started for everyone: no chores for the kids and no cooking or cleaning for Mom since Aunt Kitty had always brought her hired help. We loved being spoiled. I wanted to live that way all the time. I envied the beautiful house and cabin, my cousin Kay's fashionable clothes, and their three cars.

Mom didn't seem envious of any of the material things. She enjoyed the socializing and the relaxation. I never considered, then, how much of a workload she had as a farmer's wife, a mother, a homemaker, and eventually, a teacher.

As many times as we made those trips, though, I did not fully grasp the lifestyle of my Southern relatives until Kay's wedding in 1957.

I was twelve years old. The springtime wedding was a pinnacle on the social calendar of "who's who." Only Mom and I attended. She fretted over what to wear—something fancy but not too much. "Elegant," she said. I was assigned the task of pouring punch for the kids at the reception. My dress had to be formal, not like anything I owned. We compromised on a navy taffeta dress with a short jacket. When we arrived in Atlanta, though, Nana seemed to think my dress looked "too wintry." Kay phoned someone who showed up with a beautiful light blue formal, full-skirted with layers of netting and tiny satin spaghetti straps. Reluctantly, I tried it on. With my shoulders bare, I felt naked. Tears welled. Mom stepped in. "I'm sure if she wears the dress we brought without the jacket, it will be fine," she said.

There were hundreds of people at the wedding. Some arrived in shiny black limousines like the ones on television. The church was packed with well-dressed guests of all ages. Fragrant white flowers adorned the altar and music from the oversized pipe organ echoed through the church. A few girls who appeared to be my age had on dresses similar to the one Kay had selected for me. As Kay strolled down the aisle with handsome Uncle Harllee, she glanced from side to side, smiling at everyone until she caught my eye and winked.

The Piedmont Drive-In Club hosted the reception. Ice statues with bowls of shrimp broke up the banquet room, waiters in white jackets served champagne, silver platters filled with all kinds of food lined the sides of the room, the biggest wedding cake I ever saw dominated a corner, and an orchestra played. I stood at attention behind the punch bowl and soaked up the happenings. Mom kept me company for a while. "Isn't this something?" she said.

I nodded. "Kay is beautiful. I wish I'd worn the dress she picked," I said, feeling suddenly very out of place.

"You look perfect. I'm as proud of you as Aunt Kitty is of Kay," she said. I found that hard to believe, but I wanted to. Usually she was critical of my preteen appearance and especially so when we visited Atlanta.

*   *   *

When I was growing up, Christmas was the biggest deal of the year in Ohio, and our family traditions were eagerly observed in the same manner each holiday season. Right after Thanksgiving, which we always had at Uncle Walter's, Mom started baking cookies and shopped for perfect gifts for the aunts and uncles. We decorated the house and hung our handmade stockings at the mantel. Two weeks before Christmas, we bought a tree and decorated it together as a family. Dad usually sat and sipped tea. He became what he called sidewalk superintendent while the rest of us pulled out the collection of decorations, lights, and tinsel. Many of the ornaments were made by Lilly or our Aunt Esther and had our names on them. With the freshly cut tree and all the garlands Mom put around the fireplace and doorways, the house smelled of pine for weeks. I remember when the Craddocks, our closest neighbor a quarter mile away, were the first to buy a plastic tree. We thought it was terrible. "It won't smell like Christmas," Richie said.

By Christmas Eve, we children were too excited to sleep. Mom frequently gave us a sleeping pill (baby aspirin), with the promise that Santa wouldn't come until we slept. When we woke, the traditional sheet covered the archway into the living room to block our view. We were not allowed in there until Dad had finished milking and we had eaten breakfast together. It seemed like Dad always wanted extra toast and coffee those mornings. After the drama of the wait, he'd announce for us to get ready. We would scurry to the top of the stairs while he and Mom removed the sheet, turned on the Christmas lights, and took their seats . . . Dad in the black rocker and Mom in the overstuffed green chair. "Okay, c'mon down!" was the signal. It's a wonder Sally wasn't trampled in the fury. Each of us rushed to our own stack of presents from Santa and from the Atlanta relatives. "Don't forget, we'll take turns opening gifts," Dad would insist.

Mom usually raved about her presents from us. "I needed bath powder so bad," she might exclaim in the most sincere voice. Dad was a different story. He had to be coaxed. He routinely inspected, shook and then guessed the contents of a gift box. "Shirt," he'd say and then put it down, unopened, and laugh. It wasn't that he was so hard to please as he was hard to impress. Until Christmas, 1957.

We had opened all our gifts and everyone helped clean up scraps of torn paper, careful to pick out reusable ribbon and boxes. Mom busied herself in the kitchen, frequently peering out the window. Suddenly a revved engine noise came from the driveway. We heard the dog barking up a storm.

"Rich, I do have one last thing for you. Grab your coat and come with me." We ran to the back door and stood in our pajamas as they headed toward a man on a motorcycle. I squinted, then realized it was Jim Venus, a neighbor.

We saw Mom and Dad talking but we couldn't hear a thing. Mom pointed toward the bike. Dad smiled, shook his head, and then kissed her. He shook his head some more and circled the bike. The two of them laughed and laughed. So did Jim Venus.

After Dad's test drive, Dad rolled the bike into the shed and they strolled into the house holding hands. We all gathered around in the living room.

"How in the heck did you pull that off?" Dad said.

Mom giggled like a person does when they're proud of something they just did. "We all saw Jim ride by on his motorcycle from time to time, right?" she said. "I called him to see if he could give me some pointers, and he ended up saying he'd sell me his bike. He said he'd make me a really good deal."

Dad grinned. "And what was that?"

"He said two hundred dollars. I said I couldn't afford that and started to hang up. He asked what I could afford and I told him a hundred. And he took it."

Dad liked that story as much as the motorcycle.

In contrast, I don't remember Mom getting personal gifts from Dad. He bought her things like household appliances and electric blankets. But on their anniversary Dad wrote poetry. On the big day, he'd get the number of roses that corresponded to the number of years they'd been married. He'd clip a piece of paper with a sentence on each rose and number them in order. His carefully chosen words proved thoughtful consideration. But I wondered why he didn't just buy a card—it would have been so much easier. Each year, Mom read the poem to us out loud as she took each verse off a rose. She cried every time. We usually groaned or moved into the living room to watch television.

"He was more sentimental than anyone knew," Mom said years later.

The year I was in sixth grade, the rural community where we lived needed teachers for Chatham elementary school. Mr. Burlingame, the principal, learned that Mom had three years of college at the University of Georgia, so he visited her to see if she would consider taking a job. I overheard Dad say he thought it would be good for her, but I didn't know until years later that he'd also said, "It's the only way we can make a go of it."

Mr. Burlingame arranged for Mom to receive a temporary teaching certificate, conditioned upon her return to college locally to complete her degree. That translated to her teaching during the school year and taking two college courses each summer. She took the classes seriously and reported on various professors with admiration. More than once she said, "I'm saving money for you kids to go to college."

Mom's first friend at the school was my teacher, Mrs. Parish (Helen). I worried whenever they talked, immediately suspicious they were talking about me. Apparently, they rarely did. Gossip, a shared appreciation for new ideas in education, and the ineptitude of the new principal who had replaced Burlingame gave them plenty of other topics to discuss. They quickly discovered a mutual love of adventure, the arts, and music. Often they planned trips to hear the Cleveland Orchestra, catch an art exhibit, or tour a famous garden. We were just glad Mom had someone to go with her so we wouldn't have to. In addition to Alta from church, Mom began to develop a network of working women friends.

Dad asked lots of questions about Mom's work. Unlike the tales I tried to tell him about my high school, he seemed to love the stories she told at dinner of her second graders' antics. It seemed more like another part of her life rather than a job. We all pitched in here and there with doing dishes, vacuuming, or straightening things up around the house. She made such a big deal over any little thing we did for her, and we liked the attention. Lilly taught me how to iron and make pies. Not many of my friends had mothers who worked outside the home, and it made me proud of her to have that distinction. Mom seemed able to juggle it without complaint or incident. She told me years later that teaching reminded her of the only other job she had at Southern Bell during the war. She said it gave her pride to do something for herself and to make money.

Except for the opinions voiced by Nana. Mom kept the fact that she was going to teach from Nana for several months, until Dad insisted she tell her. "Get it over with, if you think it's going to be a problem. She'll find out anyhow," he said.

When Mom told her, she got the reaction she feared. Nana vehemently objected, first by phone and then by mail. Nana's rationale was that after a full day of teaching, Mom wouldn't have any patience left for her own children. The fact that Mom and Dad needed the money for their future didn't seem to matter to her. Nana continued to voice her disapproval for several years, but Mom wouldn't argue. She just listened even though I could tell it made her mad.

We all witnessed right from the start how much Mom liked teaching. She always had a soft spot for small children. I heard people talk about how good she was with kids and I wondered what she did that made her so good.

I knew she liked to tell the kids stories from her childhood and from the farm as rewards for good classroom behavior or for getting through their schoolwork. As popular as Dr. Seuss was, the children preferred her stories and they had their favorites: "Tell us the one about you and Clyde when you were a kid at the swimming hole and the dog jumped in, or the one about Richie and Nancy when they camped out in the orchard and foxes circled the tent," they begged.

The first couple of years teaching second grade Mom learned just how much poverty existed in our community. Oil had been struck many years earlier in the small town, but it turned out to be a fluke. Abandoned drills and oil-crusted dirt piles littered the countryside. Many residents struggled to put food on the table, let alone dress their children in their finest for a Christmas pageant, an annual tradition begun by Mom and Helen. As the pageant drew near, Mom began gathering up and distributing unused clothing from our closets, so no one in her class would be embarrassed by not having a special outfit to wear. Once she brought the poorest children, a twin boy and girl, to our house so they could bathe, have clean hair, and a hot meal before the performance. The transformation was so profound not even their own father recognized them when he picked them up.

For the pageant, Mom played the piano, and Helen developed the theme by which each grade performed a song, skit, or played simple instruments. The finale was always a play in which the best talent from all six grades participated. The first big production I remember was a reenactment of the *Three Billy Goat's Gruff*. Mom and Helen cast Smokey Joe, a child from Mom's second grade class, in the lead. They might have worried over casting someone so young, but I'd heard all the funny stories about the Norman Rockwell type boy at our dinner table . . . his cute face, a smattering of freckles across his nose and cheek, missing front teeth and a lisp, which put his classmates in hysterics. "When my new teeth grows back, you guys won't be laughing. I'll be beautiful," Smokey Joe supposedly said once as he slicked his hands over his head.

That night, Smokey played the troll whose famous line was, "Who's that trip-trappin' over my bridge?" The line was repeated three times as each of the billy goats illegally used the bridge. Smokey's r's became w's, and he got bigger and bigger laughs each time he yelled it out. Mom and Helen had chosen their lead well.

*   *   *

The teaching job gave Mom and Dad a little breathing room, financially speaking. Though it appeared they discussed every financial decision, I never heard Mom disagree with anything Dad wanted. She'd smile and say if he thought it was what they needed to do, then it was okay with her. Later on, I might catch her alone, staring out the window like someone does when they're deep in thought or worried. It seemed like Dad bought everything on his list. Meanwhile, she had the same bedroom furniture, hand-me-down living and dining room pieces from Lilly, carpets she had sewn together to fit the room, no garage for the car, and new clothes for us but not her. "I have everything I need," she said when I asked her what she wanted.

Mom should have worried about our frequent Sunday afternoon trips to Cleveland Hopkins Airport. Dad would park outside the airport fence, close to the runways, where we all watched the airplanes take off and land. As a novelty we enjoyed it, but we soon tired of the whole thing. Maybe Mom did too, but she didn't show it. Sometimes Dad bribed us with, "Ten more minutes and I'll take you to Dairy Queen. Okay?" He always had us with that one. We kids thought we were at the airport just to watch, never dreaming that Dad contemplated actually buying an airplane. Mom recently admitted she never suspected either. She also said that once Dad broached the subject, she objected, for the first and only time. They discussed it for months. He, I think, plied her with the notion that she'd be able to see her relatives (in Atlanta and Iowa) more often and that the two of them could fly to Cleveland and dine in the fancy restaurant at the airport. She told me she didn't really believe any of that but she finally gave in anyway. Dad wanted a plane so badly, and she wanted him to be happy. "He needed more things than I did to be satisfied," she said.

In the fall of my eighth grade we got a used Cessna 172. From the start, the single-engine plane scared me to death. Even on a smooth ride the airplane frequently dropped thirty or forty feet in altitude unexpectedly and made me think we were going to crash. The noise of the engine, the tight quarters, strong gasoline smell, the constant beep-beeping of the radio and reoccurrence of my motion sickness did nothing to delight me in having such a luxury. Every announcement of an upcoming trip sent me reeling to the bathroom for practice. Dad accused me of having an active imagination, even though I usually did throw up. I'm not sure if Mom really liked the plane or not but she never seemed scared. And she never got sick. She said she trusted Dad completely. Trust had nothing to do with it for me.

Dad loved to go up by himself and buzz the farm. Sometimes I watched and wondered if he was reliving his navy days. Sally had the most fun going with him. She thrilled with the dives and had a much stronger stomach than any of us. If the neighbors stood outside their homes, Dad buzzed them too. Eventually all of the neighbors flew with him. Most of them had never been in an airplane and probably thought it to be their only opportunity. Months after we got the plane, even Lilly asked for a ride. She fidgeted all the way to the small airport. We went just to see if she'd really go. I wanted to see how Dad would fit her stout frame in the front seat, but they managed. The flight lasted five minutes. Dad told us later she never let go of the shoulder strap and begged to go back to the airport.

No matter how little Dad was able to instill his love of flying into any of us, I never saw him happier. The airplane seemed to brighten his spirit. It gave him such a thrill that I wondered on occasion if I missed something. Even when I gave it another try the sickness persisted. Dad told me that he, too, had suffered with air-sickness when he learned to fly in the navy. That surprised me. He said it eventually went away and that if I stuck with it the same thing would happen to me. But my patience wore out before my stomach strengthened.

*   *   *

In 1959 Mom turned forty. She didn't receive any big gifts like an airplane or anything. Instead, Dad and Lilly planned a surprise birthday party for the big day. He told us kids about the party, insisted each of us write a poem, and gave us money to buy gifts. Invited guests were Lilly, Aunt Sis and John, Alta, Helen, Mom's friend Vennetta and her husband Elmer, plus our farm neighbors. He and Lilly talked on the phone about the party every time Mom left the house. It seemed like they worked on it for weeks. Dad had never done anything like this before, and he was excited but nervous.

Lilly threw fun parties all the time. She usually had dips for potato chips, walnut cheese balls and Ritz crackers, pigs-in-a-blanket, Swedish meatballs, tiny egg salad sandwiches, and a cake from Hough Bakery. I knew that if Lilly helped Dad, it would be special. Dad stressed that he wanted Mom to be surprised. He emphasized it the most to me.

"Nancy, you be careful. I know how hard it is for you to keep a secret. Don't spoil the fun, okay?"

The day of the party, Mom was quiet. There was none of her usual laughter. I wanted her to be happy. I didn't know how to comfort her, but I didn't say a word about the party. Later in the afternoon I walked into the bathroom and caught Mom staring in front of the mirror as she inspected her hair. She scowled. I must have given her a puzzled look.

"I'm old now, Nancy. Gray hair everywhere," she said as her eyes teared up.

"You look younger than any of my friends' mothers," I said. "And Dad says you're as pretty as the day he married you."

She smiled. "Maybe a bubble bath would cheer me up. Ohio in February is such a bad month for a birthday. It's so cold and dreary."

I closed the door and scurried to find Dad. I wondered if we should tell her about the party. He didn't seem worried. He said she'd be fine and to just give her some time alone.

When Mom finished in the bathroom, Dad showered and changed clothes. I worried she would think that was odd because he never showered in the middle of the day. If she suspected anything, she sure didn't show it. Dad asked her to go with him into Lodi to look at something. As soon as they got out of the house, Lilly arrived. She had bags of food, champagne, flowers, and a beautiful cake. She gave all three of us kids jobs to do. She hummed while she set up the dining room table and arranged flowers. I stood back, amazed at how quickly the ordinary room was transformed into something special. The other guests began to fill the house. Everyone brought gifts. Richie made everyone park their cars behind the barn so Mom wouldn't suspect a thing until the last minute.

"Surprise!" we all yelled as my parents returned home. Mom smiled, laughed, and cried all at once. Her look told me she hadn't suspected a thing. She raved on and on about how "we shouldn't have," but I think she was glad we did.

It was a week or so after the party, at supper, when Dad glanced over at her. "Peter didn't call this year," he said. "Hmm."

Mom shrugged her shoulders like it hadn't occurred to her. Her blasé attitude made me believe she didn't care a bit.

Part II

Elise in Atlanta

Remembering back, 2005

My mother and Peter stand in front of Nana's house on South Prado Street in Ansley Park, where Mom spent her teenage and young-adult years. Looking at the yellowed photograph, I can barely make out the number forty-one over Peter's shoulder, but of course I know the house. Perched on a hill with a sloping roofline toward the street, its architecture is more cottage than Southern. It is only once you are inside that you realize the bulk of the house comes from its depth. Shrubs flank the twosome as they perch atop the steep concrete steps that lead from the sidewalk to the front door. I remember how fatigued I was—as a child—whenever I climbed them.

In the picture, Peter wears baggy trousers and a long-sleeved shirt open at the neck, his thick hair combed straight back. He stands close to my mother without touching, staring worshipfully at her, rather than looking at the person taking the picture. Mom has on a long pleated skirt, a sweater, and a pearl necklace. Her shoulder-length hair falls in soft finger waves.

As we sit together in 2005, Mom watches me inspect this rare souvenir that she only recently unearthed.

"You're both so thin," I blurt out before considering how impolite it sounds.

She laughs, not offended. "It was 1940, when we were twenty-one and before gravity took over."

Sixty-five years later, I'm still taking in details about their relationship from over sixty years before—a history that is grounded mainly in stories, but occasionally in a shred of physical evidence, like this photo.

"It's the only picture I have of the two of us," she says softly. I want to ask why, but I don't. She told me once that she returned all of Peter's pictures and other memorabilia when she broke up with him. Peter probably destroyed the bulk of it.

I am visiting Mom in Atlanta on a sweltering July day. As familiar as I am with the story of her early years and her love affair with Peter, each time we are together, Mom remembers something new. Sometimes the catalyst is a song she hasn't heard in a long time. Sometimes we drive down an Atlanta street she hasn't been on in a while, and a building or street name jogs a memory. The added information is always revealing and fascinating to me, even though she usually prefaces the comment with, "This probably isn't important . . ."

I give her time to reflect, careful not to interrupt with questions. The longer I wait, the more she elaborates, making me feel like a good psychologist who lets the patient do all the talking. As open as my mother is about most subjects, she is private about her deepest feelings—I'm only beginning to understand just how much.

Mom pours me another glass of iced tea as we sit at the kitchen table. I glance up at her and then back to the photo. "Too bad this isn't in color—we could compare your natural hair with L'Oreal."

She waves her hand at me. "It's still red. Bob just does highlights."

"Ma, you're eighty-two. Your hair doesn't exist on a color chart anywhere," I say.

My siblings and I tend to be long on teasing, a trait we probably picked up from Dad. She knows this and even laughs about it. It's easy to fall into this familiar pattern, but I want to change my bad habit, before it's too late to let her know how much I admire her. I know I've never said enough.

I reach out and take her hand in mine. "You look great. All that swimming, walking, and dancing paid off," I say. "I'll bet no one ever guesses your age." She smiles at the last part.

All of the stories I've heard over the years from Mom, her old Atlanta friends, and from family members start flooding back to me. I picture how she might have been before meeting my father, before my birth. When she was just Elise.

*   *   *

I imagine my mother as a vacation accident, given that her siblings, Kitty and Chase, were twelve and fourteen years older than she. Back in those days, Nana and Pops looked forward to their annual spring vacation. Perhaps Nana stopped saying, "Not now, C.P." the way she usually did whenever Pops tried to kiss her in front of anyone. Yet her undemonstrative nature belied the deep devotion and strong feelings that made Kitty and Chase wonder just what went on when the bedroom door closed.

No one can venture a guess as to how Nana came by her ultra-conservative demeanor. Perhaps it had been instilled by her father, a Presbyterian minister. Nana's mother wasn't dull at all, though. Aunt Kitty wrote a family memoir in 1995 and described her grandmother as, " . . . gay, vivacious, and adored by all her grandchildren. Her fund of folk songs and lullabies was endless, and we used to keep her singing to us until she lost her voice. Her vivid imagination and sparkling personality made the bedtime stories she spun for us exciting and beautifully told with the dreamy qualities that rivaled Grimm."

Indeed, most of the Hunter clan (Pops, Kitty, my mother) exuded a warm, Southern gentility that endeared them to anyone they met. Nana, however, did not share their social enthusiasm and grace. She wilted in a group, quieted around strangers, and preferred to judge from the sidelines. Her matronly dress, erect posture, and thick legs added to an image of a severe critic. Mom saw Nana as shy—not truly aloof or cold—and thought Pops interested her precisely because of his easy, outgoing nature. "She wanted to be more like that," Mom has said. "And Pops, being the caring husband, drew her out in a non-threatening way."

As a child, I didn't have this insight into why Nana seemed cold—I simply respected Nana the way you do when you know someone is in charge. Though she spanked me for inappropriate behavior her tongue-lashings frightened me more. And I hated the ensuing silent treatment the most. With Mom and Dad, we were spanked and then kissed. That meant even the worst storm ended in minutes, and then forgotten. Nana took a more severe approach, perhaps because she saw her role more as substitute parent than grandparent. It didn't help that we compared everything she did to our other grandmother, Lilly, who loved us unconditionally and always gathered us up into her arms. The only time I witnessed that kind of physical affection from Nana was when her great-grandchildren were babies. Seeing her cuddle and kiss them made me realize that Nana adored the infants and that she must have welcomed her own unexpected pregnancy in middle age.

The forty-something parents eagerly anticipated their "gift from God." Pops' wiry frame and baldness, along with Nana's gray hair confused strangers after the baby arrived. Many mistook the two for grandparents.

Neither seemed upset by the error—Pops laughed and joked that he couldn't remember when he had hair, while Nana simply shrugged her right shoulder.

They had more time to spend with my mother than they had with their first two children, and they lavished attention upon Elise. Even though raised as an only child, she never became a spoiled brat.

Aunt Kitty once wrote in a letter to me, "Despite what Chase and I feared, Elise grew up with a sweet disposition and generous spirit, which has remained. Her affectionate nature endeared her not only to her parents but to everyone."

Mom idolized Nana at an early age. Her siblings said if she wasn't holding Nana's hand, she wanted to sit on her lap and be read to, or plop down in the garden while Nana worked on the flower beds.

"We both preferred the outdoors. It became our special time together when she taught me the names of flowers and birds," Mom said.

Until she mentioned that ten years ago, I never considered how much Mom's relationship with Nana mirrored the one she had later with her own youngest child. Mom and Sally each had a desire to be close, almost dependent, upon their mothers.

Nana doted on her pretty little girl. She wound Elise's thick, red tresses around a rod every night before bed, and the bouncy curls became a magnet for admiration.

Nana also loved to dress Mom in smocked dresses and outfits. She labored over her Singer sewing machine as she copied clothes from magazines or fine department stores, always without a pattern. Her great care to inside seams and her elaborate embroidery made them one of a kind. Mom liked getting dressed up, and she enjoyed the attention her mother gave to make every outfit just right. Despite Nana's straight-laced decorum, she kept up on the latest fashions and knew exactly how to tie hair ribbons for the perfect finishing touch.

While Mom learned domestic skills from Nana, she developed a love for athletics from Pops, who remained an avid tennis player and sportsman. During the summer months, young Elise and the neighbor boy, Clyde, met Pops at the streetcar as he returned from work and begged him to take them swimming at Moseley Park. Truthfully, not much begging ensued since Pops couldn't wait to go himself. The threesome swam, splashed, and dove. Pops loved the water and taught Elise to swim by age four. Nana usually accompanied them, only to sit on a bench and watch, and eventually announce "Time to go." No one knows why she never learned to swim.

It certainly wasn't a fear of water, since she adored boat rides. Perhaps the bathing suit seemed risqué for her taste.

Pops and Nana also had a deep, abiding faith that they passed on to Mom, who learned from their example about the inner peace and strength that prayer provided. The family attended church religiously: Pops taught Sunday school each week while Nana played the piano. Mom has said she felt as if she lived at the church on Sunday, given the routine of Sunday school, church service, and then returning to the church on Sunday evening for a kind of Bible study. Despite the rigor of the schedule, she looked upon it as a whole day spent with her parents, except for Sunday afternoons when Nana and Pops disappeared into their bedroom for a long nap (perhaps where Mom got the idea for how to spend Sunday afternoons in her own married life).

The Great Depression did not impact Mom's comfortable and idyllic life: Pops bought his first car when Elise was young, numerous and grand Christmas gifts piled up under the tree, and the household always employed help.

"I knew my parents were thrifty," Mom has told me. "But I don't remember a single instance when we went without."

As he left for work each day, Pops declared, "I hope we don't have to close the bank today." He said it so often that, eventually, no one took his offhand remark seriously, but no one ever joked about it either. The bank remained solvent, and that allowed Mom's family to weather the Depression unscathed.

In fact, when Mom was fourteen, the family moved from Atlanta's West End to a newer house in the upscale Ansley Park neighborhood. She cried for days, convinced she would never see Clyde or her best friend Louise again. (In actuality, the girls remained in contact for the rest of their lives.) Eventually, Mom accepted the move in a more positive light. She didn't mope or whine. "A good cry always works magic for me," she told me many times before I appreciated the wisdom in that belief.

She came to appreciate their tasteful new home: a careful smattering of antiques—including Nana's dining room table and a sideboard with a thick marble top—added a sense of history and lore to the more modern house. Mom's favorite room turned out to be the oversized screened-in porch on the backside of the house that overlooked a fish pond and tiered flower beds. Nana prided herself on the colorful and lush gardens, thick with pink azaleas, paper whites, and hyacinth. Two magnolia trees and one dogwood shaded the area closest to the house. It created a pleasing visual effect and the yard exuded the most wonderful scents for most of the year.

All in all, Mom enjoyed a harmonious upbringing, if sheltered. She respected her parents' rules and followed them without debate or question. Only once did she receive a spanking—for going to a neighbor girl's house without asking for permission.

"Nana insisted that Pops give me a swat," she told me. "It took him so long to spank me, I felt sorry for him."

Along the way Mom decided that her parents knew best in *all* matters. Perhaps the protective upbringing made her less confident in her own opinions, or maybe she simply reflected the values of the times in her respect for and duty to family. Nonetheless, her loyalty to family extended to friends, as she valued long-term friendships.

Nana and Mom's bond remained sealed into her adulthood—their unwavering devotion to one another lasted a lifetime. I cannot fathom such unconditional love and adoration. It must have buoyed up Nana as much as it tested her resolve about Mom's future. I ponder if Nana ever regretted her responsibility or her role in the outcome.

*   *   *

1940-1942

In high school, Elise fell in with a tight group of friends: Eugenia, Emily, Ida, the Eatin' boys (Harrison and Paul, who ate nonstop), Wink, Jimmie and Hack. She made new girlfriends and liked many of the boys, although she was never comfortable one-on-one. The crowd went on group dates, which were the norm then, and the high schools were divided by sex: Boys High School and Girls High School. This resulted in a quite naïve Elise when it came to romantic relationships. The whole gang would meet at the movie theater, and afterwards they might go to Piedmont Park to sit on the edge of the lake and play cards. It was all innocent fun—no one in the gang coupled up except for Eugenia and Jimmie, several years after high school. Initially, not even college deterred their friendships.

The last member to join the entourage was Peter. By then most of the gang attended the University of Georgia extension, a two-year program similar to a junior college. Often, the crowd met at the student union over the lunch hour and danced to records or stood around the piano and listened to Wink play. Eugenia shared an English class with Peter and one day invited him to meet the others.

As Eugenia tells it, Peter joined the group on a marvelous spring day. Wink played his version of "String of Pearls," while everyone hummed along. Notes and rhythm pulsed in his bloodstream. "You should do this for a living instead of studying to be a pharmacist," Hack yelled out.

Peter entered the union, caught a familiar eye, and headed for the group. After he met everyone, he moved around the piano and stood next to Elise. "You look so familiar. I mean redheads are as memorable as they are rare. Have we met before?" he said.

Elise took a step back. "I'm sure we haven't," she said.

Even though all the friends could tell Elise found him attractive, he *was* a little forward. Maybe his devilish remarks excited her, or maybe she admired his confidence.

"Shame to waste this good music—care to dance?" Peter said.

Elise blushed and took his hand. His slender physique, thick brown hair, full lips, and hazel eyes intrigued her. Peter twirled her around, stepped out, and then pulled her back into his arms with ease. He danced with his whole body and made it look effortless and graceful. His fingers spread into her lower back and he guided her in the direction he wanted her to go while his arms gently pulled her along. Wink increased the volume as the couple sailed by. All conversation stopped as everyone watched. When they came off the dance floor, yelps and whistles filled the room. "Just met, huh?" Wink blurted out and went right into "I've Got My Eyes on You."

Peter fell hard. Elise sensed stirrings of something that she couldn't quite identify. She had never been in love before, so it was new for her.

"And what a dancer!" Mom has said. "Never before had I met someone who danced better than I could and had so much fun. But more than the dancing, I felt an easy connection, like we'd known each other forever."

At school, the two became inseparable. Overnight, Elise blossomed into woman as her bearing went from fun and friendships to thoughts about a man, having a family, and thinking of herself in a whole new way. Within a week or so, Peter arrived at the family home to pick up Elise for a movie date.

"So pleased to meet you, Mr. Hunter and Mrs. Hunter," he said eagerly. Peter looked Pops square in the eye and shook his hand with confidence.

Pops outgoing personality made getting to know him a breeze, and in turn, he enjoyed meeting new people and learning about them. He had a soft spot for young men just starting out, remembering (perhaps) his own early days. Pops and Peter warmed to each other in minutes. They even shared a love of jokes and puns, something they quickly discovered.

"I like him," Pops said later to the family. "He'll go places."

Nana was not similarly impressed. On that day, she gave Peter an up-and-down look and then shrugged her right shoulder as a kind of dismissal, a habit that had become her trademark. Maybe his glibness rubbed her the wrong way. Perhaps she struggled with her daughter's transformation into a young woman, and she worried about Elise dancing the night away in Peter's arms. Nana possibly subscribed to the belief that dancing was nothing more than a vertical position for a horizontal desire.

Elise, embarrassed at Nana's dismissal, tried to gloss over it. Peter laughed. He shuffled his feet like he was trying to find solid ground in quicksand.

"Chilly in there, down right chilly," he joked once they got outside.

"Mother is really a lovely person. You'll see," Elise promised.

*   *   *

From the start, the twosome had much in common: similar tastes in music, a love of the water, an appreciation of books, and a deep faith. They talked and talked—though Peter often steered the conversation, as he stubbornly adhered to his beliefs and opinions, while Elise expressed herself with more reticence.

The couple often enjoyed a favorite walk to Piedmont Park, circling the lake and stopping to watch the ducks glide across the water. They worried about the threat of war, which everyone said was imminent. People still talked about World War I and the devastation it had wrought. No justification existed for a less onerous war.

At the time, Peter didn't fear being drafted into the U.S. Army, even though the popular song "Goodbye dear, I'll Be Back in a Year," reflected people's assumptions. Men accepted service in the armed forces as their duty and obligation."

Because Peter had worked for the phone company, he was qualified for the Signal Corps, which took men right after they completed boot camp. The assignments didn't involve being on the front lines, or in dangerous places. Plus, he figured the army experience would make him more valuable after the war.

"So none of the troops worried after World War II started?" I asked him in one of my interviews.

He shook his head and paused. "Well, I can't speak for the pilots. The statistic of one died every thirteen minutes must have been hard to hear."

Despite the specter of war, the couple intensified their relationship, and Elise started to spread her wings from her protective mother. In the 1940s, it was unusual for a twenty-year-old to have his own automobile (Peter's salary of sixteen dollars a week from his job with Southern Bell went a long way toward paying off his little red Ford and his college tuition). Nana worried about the two of them driving all over town, alone. Nana, who clung stubbornly to old-fashioned morality, even wished to enforce the no-dancing decree of the Presbyterian church on her daughter. Luckily for Elise, Kitty stepped in on her behalf.

"Times have changed, mother," Kitty told her. "Everyone dances now, not just the Methodists."

Nana relented, possibly feeling some guilt over forbidding Kitty to dance when she was young. While her friends attended dances Kitty had been sequestered in her room, where she usually curled up with a book. It wasn't until Kitty's sophomore year in college that her older brother, Chase, announced that Kitty would be his date for a dance. Nana never quibbled with Chase. Kitty beamed but fright overcame her. "Don't worry sister, I'll teach you," he assured her.

Elise cherished the times Kitty stood up for her, since she herself never argued with Nana, no matter how painful the conflict. When Kitty stood up to Nana, she usually won, which made an impression on Elise. Kitty used her bullets sparingly because she only argued if she felt strongly.

While Nana remained worried about her daughter's growing feelings for Peter, Pops expressed genuine interest in Peter's future plans and encouraged him to talk openly about them. His ambitious plans included a college degree and success in business, as well as a house in Buckhead. Peter was the first boy in his family to go to college: he worked all day as a cable splicer and attended the University of Georgia night school. Pops said Peter's parents must be proud at such a big step. These were not words of courtesy but came from his heartfelt belief in education as the key to success. Pops opened up to Peter about his own college experiences with academia and how he met Nana.

"Being a student came easy for me, so easy I finished Peabody College in three years," he said, "not that I'm here to brag." He chuckled out of embarrassment as he scratched his bald head. "But I liked to visit with my friends and have fun, too. But no woman impressed me until I saw her." He pointed at Nana. She flushed.

Peter asked Pops to continue. He couldn't imagine what any man would have seen in Nana or even imagine her as a looker, as Pops implied. "I saw one tough old bird," he said.

Pops looked away, like he enjoyed a pleasant thought. "She was a serious student and had a regal way about her. Good posture and wonderful skin. I had to introduce myself but she remained cool in the beginning," Pops said.

Peter had to choke back an "amen" as he glanced over at Nana. But he controlled himself and encouraged Pops to go on.

"I think I asked her if I could carry her books. Yes sir, that's how it all started," Pops said as he let out a big laugh, the kind that suggests a private memory.

"C.P.," Nana said as she turned to her husband. "Let's not bore the young people with all this recollecting."

Elise and Peter also shared a bit of a funny bone. Sometimes, they joined Pops next to the radio and listened to *Amos 'n Andy* or *Fibber McGee and Molly*. They laughed until they cried.

"Oh, that was a good one," Pops said many times as he slapped his knee. After one of those episodes, Peter did his Donald Duck imitation. Elise laughed meekly, at first perhaps embarrassed by the childish humor that so tickled her no matter how many times Peter did it. Rather quickly Pop's face reddened from laughter.

Finally Pops settled down and wiped his eyes. "Peter my boy, you know that Charles Lamb is my favorite author, right?" Peter nodded. "As a serious writer, Charles didn't appreciate puns. Supposedly the story goes that a friend accused him of jealousy, saying he couldn't compose one. A wager took place and the friend locked Charles in his library to await the outcome. Within minutes Charles banged on the door and yelled, 'O-pun the door!'"

Peter giggled, and Pops roared. Elise smiled out of courtesy, never much of a fan of puns.

Weeks turned into months and Peter relaxed around the family. Occasionally, he held Elise's hand in front of Nana and Pops. Nana frequently stared at their entwined fingers until Peter let go, but Pops didn't seem to notice, or if so he didn't care.

"On her best days, I'd say she was civil. Never better than that. I accepted it," Peter's shoulders drooped with sorrow when he recounted the incident to me as if it had just happened instead of decades earlier. "I didn't really have any choice. I loved Elise, and I decided to be patient."

*   *   *

Peter and Elise drove all over Atlanta for entertainment. They explored new theaters and parks—and they even drifted toward Lover's Leap to view the city lights. On one of those nights the pair listened to station WSB on the radio when Frank Sinatra's "From the Bottom of My Heart" came on.

"He's got such a dreamy voice but they say he's such a bad boy," Elise said.

"Frank's not so bad, just women trouble," Peter said.

"All those girls screaming and throwing themselves at him. I'll bet he hates it." Elise stroked his hand and laid her head back on the seat.

Peter eyed her thinking at first she made a joke. "I assure you, he doesn't."

Peter and Elise dated for five months before Elise had dinner with Peter's family. His parents, Frank and Ethel, differed from her parents, both in appearance and education. Frank had a burly, brusque manner and spoke in sentence fragments, while Ethel had an earthy nature—neither educated nor refined but pleasant enough. Elise didn't have a clue how to relate, but she never shared her discomfort with Peter.

Peter was the middle of five children, all of whom—(except the youngest girl)—had such similar features that you knew right away they were related. Oddly, the youngest with her blonde hair and fair skin looked as if she came from another family altogether.

The brother closest to Peter's age, Re, quickly established himself as Elise's favorite. His soft-spoken voice and engaging smile charmed her. "How did you get that name?" Elise asked at her first dinner with Peter's clan.

Re chuckled. "Mama says as a toddler I began to do everything just like Peter had done. As I grew up, he and I looked more and more alike, including talking and mannerisms. One day she said to Dad that they didn't have a Sterling, my real name, but a Re-Pete. Soon it shortened to *Re*."

Elise sat back and studied the two. "You do look like twins. Pete and Re-pete."

The boisterous household screamed with disorganization. Elise pretended to enjoy herself, but deep down she couldn't imagine being a part of Peter's family. She cringed as one of Nana's words flashed into her mind: "common."

Peter started talking about his plans for them—how they'd marry and be happy for the rest of their lives. Elise dreamed about it, too, but worried about Nana as well as her own misgivings about Peter's family.

Sometimes they would study together, although Peter as the more serious student tutored Elise in science and math. He grasped those subjects without effort. Elise, on the other hand, favored literature and shared her opinions about various authors.

"What can you do with literature or English?" Peter teased. "Will it buy us a house in Buckhead?"

Elise laughed. "I don't need that."

"But you deserve it," Peter said.

Even as Peter and Elise's lives became more intertwined, Nana held steady. There had been no change in her lack of acceptance of him. She staunchly refused to discuss anything to do with the relationship.

Why didn't Nana simply forbid Elise to see him? Did she figure her forbiddance would be the sure fire way to seal their relationship? Did she think they might elope? No matter how many times Elise asked why Nana didn't like him, she never gave any answer other than "He'll never make you happy." As months passed, Nana made everyone uncomfortable with her silence. And as much as Pops liked Peter, and loved Elise, he never opposed his wife.

"What is it, exactly, that she dislikes about me?" Peter finally asked Elise.

"Mother says you'll never make me happy," she said. "But I know you will."

I shook my head as Mom recalled the statement to me for probably the hundredth time. "So Nana never said a word?" I said. "Ever?"

"No. Nothing," she said with teary eyes.

Nevertheless, Peter tried everything to impress Nana. He noticed her gardens, naming the plants in the beds. He complimented her cooking. He asked her opinions of books she read. Nothing worked. Her standoffishness persisted.

"She'll change her mind," Peter insisted.

During this time, Peter and Elise visited Kitty and Harllee often. There, at least, they were welcomed as a couple.

Harllee told funny stories about his legal practice, boyhood, and college. His voice commanded attention and he preferred to be the only one who spoke. Peter provided a dutiful ear and the appropriate laughter. The side benefit to the one-sided exchanges was that Harllee shared advice on business and how to get ahead in a company. He seemed to be a natural businessman with his keen and introspective style.

Some time after Elise turned twenty, people began to say how much she looked like Kitty. Elise felt complimented. On one of the weekend visits, she asked Harllee if he thought so.

"I can see a resemblance. But, Elise, you're petite and cute, while Kitty is elegant and sophisticated," Harllee said. The remark hurt Elise's feelings, but Peter said Harllee didn't mean anything negative.

After more than a year of dating, Peter proposed. Elise cried. She said yes. The couple debated over how to tell Nana and Pops. In the end, they decided to tackle Nana by herself. They rehearsed a little and then called her into the living room. On a beautiful spring day in 1941, with a thick drift of dogwood blossoms the couple prepared for their announcement.

Nana sat on the edge of her chair, her back straight and eyes expressionless. The nervous couple eyed each other.

Elise stepped forward with as much inner strength as possible. She wrung her hands. "Peter has asked me to marry him and I've agreed."

Nana burst into tears. "Oh, mercy me. No!" she shouted and hurried out into the backyard. Elise gaped. She had never seen her mother cry. What had been planned as a happy day withered before her eyes. She had feared disapproval but never envisioned that reaction.

Elise persuaded Peter to leave. She hoped she alone might be able to comfort Nana. She sat for a while and probed the universe for answers, but got none. Naively, she must have reasoned that Nana only wanted happiness for her. And how could she impress upon her how much she loved Peter? And why had Nana been so surprised about the engagement when the pair had been inseparable for more than a year?

She decided to take a mild-mannered approach, trying to appeal to Nana's sense of romance and choice. She remembered that her mother had once shared that Pops was the only man she had ever loved. With all the resolve and optimism she could muster, Elise navigated toward the back door as if blindfolded.

Elise only needed to glance around the yard before spotting Nana on the glider, her foot gently pushing her back and forth in a timed cadence.

"Mother?" she said in a near whisper as she approached the glider.

Elise sat down beside her mother and took her hand, which felt cool and limp. Nana gazed straight ahead, unresponsive.

"I'm so sorry you cried. But I love him. More than I can possibly explain to you," she said as she twirled the diamond engagement ring around on her finger.

A hint of a breeze fluttered through the dogwood tree as two wrens screeched and dove playing tag, unaffected by the serious conversation below them.

"Peter is not the one. He will never make you happy. You must trust me on this," Nana said.

"How do you know, Mother?"

Nana pulled a handkerchief from her bosom and dabbed at the perspiration on her forehead.

"I just do. I know. I do not want you to marry him." She jabbed at the air with a bony finger.

*   *   *

Nana tried a new tack: she began to introduce Elise to young men whenever she could. She invited handsome Tommy Baker, who lived around the block, for dinner. Tommy was two years older than Elise and attended Davidson College. Tommy tended to Nana's chair, he praised the meal to the hilt after just one bite. He was beyond polite. Accordingly, Elise thought him nice but stiff, and she declined his invitations for a date. Nana lamented the rejection but remained undeterred in her search for an acceptable boyfriend for her youngest child.

In her despair, Elise confided in Kitty. Elise cherished her older sister and secretly wished she had Kitty's confidence and poise. She respected Kitty's advice on everything from fashion to female issues, even if her older sister often played the seniority card.

"Mother is set in her ways and opinions," Kitty said. "Don't you remember Tom Becknell?"

Elise nodded slowly as she remembered the tall, dark, handsome man Kitty had fallen deeply in love with at age twenty-one. Tom, a U.S. Navy man, had decided to become a career military man. Nana believed that wouldn't be any kind of future for her daughter and pronounced, "He'll never amount to anything."

"Did you want to marry him?" Elise probed.

Kitty never answered, but her dreamy expression made Elise wonder. Instead Kitty paused. "Mother was wrong, you know. Tom is well on his way to becoming one of the youngest admirals ever."

*   *   *

Despite Nana's misgivings, Elise and Peter remained engaged. In the early summer of 1941, Peter's parents invited Elise on a trip to St. Simon's Island off the coast of Georgia. The invitation excited Elise: she had heard wonderful things about the island and had never been there. More importantly, she'd be with Peter for seven full days and nights. Nana took a dim view of the offer. Eventually, through Elise's pleading, she relented. Peter's parents invited cousin Sarah as "company" for Elise.

High anticipation dominated the day as the family started their drive to Brunswick, Georgia, and then onto the causeway. Peter fantasized about the time he would have with Elise, not to mention the beach and cooler weather. Summer heat and humidity started early that year. "What a great idea you had, Mother," Frank said to Ethel.

Elise wondered about the affectionate term Frank used with his wife. At first she thought it odd but she shrugged it off when she realized that Ethel seemed to like it.

Everyone chatted about their plans once they arrived. Peter squeezed Elise's hand in the backseat and winked. It made her excited and a little nervous.

"Maybe you could get a sun tan," he teased.

"If I do, it'll be the first time ever," she said.

St. Simon's looked old and grand. Mature live oak trees lined the streets, and the ocean was in view from nearly everywhere they looked. They whistled in appreciation. Quite soon after they drove onto the island, Frank pointed out the two-story cottage that would be home for the week. The manicured lawn and quaint cottage had a screened-in porch that faced the water. Everyone climbed out of the car and breathed in the salty air. A soft breeze picked up as if on cue.

An exploration of the accommodations delighted everyone: a radio, record player, jigsaw puzzles, and books. Four bedrooms and two bathrooms allowed plenty of room to spread out. Each of the young people had their own room, while Frank and Ethel shared one. Peter winked at Elise as she selected the room next to his.

Frank unloaded the car while Ethel settled the kitchen. "You kids get your suits on and head to the beach," he said.

Peter initially thought his parents would want to spend time on the beach as well, but it turned out they mostly liked sitting on the porch and watching the action from afar. By the second day, they amused themselves with a 500-piece jigsaw puzzle, which they set up on a coffee table. "We have simple needs," Ethel said when Peter asked why they didn't want to take a dip in the ocean.

The seven-day trip seemed like more than enough time to relax and enjoy each other's company, and maybe even provide a chance for Elise to get to know Peter's family better—but as it happened, she didn't interact with them other than at dinner. Even Sarah all but disappeared, perhaps feeling like a third wheel. She preferred to stake out a spot on the beach where she set up a small umbrella, slathered herself with sun tan lotion, and lay completely still for hours.

Peter and Elise, happily finding themselves alone, strolled on the beach. They discovered coves and other private places where they kissed and necked in twilight. It was the closest she had ever come to having sex. Though she yearned to sleep with Peter, her fear of getting pregnant overrode emotion. Peter patiently agreed to wait until they were married.

A magical trip ended on a somber note.

Re appeared on the next-to-the-last day with an envelope for Peter. "Sorry, buddy," he said.

Peter glanced at the return address: United States government. He knew right away it held his draft notice.

Elise leaned against his shoulder. "When do you have to go?"

"Thirty days. We still have lots of time," he said.

The steady dating and engagement paused as Peter prepared to leave for the army. At the time, draftees typically served one year—unless it was war-time, in which case a tour of duty could be extended indefinitely.

Peter convinced Elise that Fort Jackson, South Carolina, wasn't that far away, and they pledged to write every day. As much as Elise saddened at the thought of Peter's impending departure, she looked forward to her upcoming junior year at University of Georgia, when she would transfer to the main campus in Athens to finish schooling. Peter told her he wished he were driving to Athens instead of wearing army boots and sleeping in barracks.

On their last date before Peter left for boot camp, the pair went to a movie and later sipped on an orange crush at the Varsity drive-in. Elise cleared her throat and then made a surprising remark.

"Do you think, maybe, we should see other people," Elise said tentatively. "Just for companionship?"

Peter scowled.

She fiddled with the collar of her blouse. "I still have your ring, of course, even though Mother probably thinks I returned it. Nothing would change between us."

He reluctantly agreed, but he didn't like the idea one bit.

On the day Peter left for Fort Jackson, Elise rode in the car with Peter, Frank, and Ethel on the way to the train station. Finally she fully grasped his leaving. The two held hands in the back seat. She cried. "Please take me with you," she said softly.

"Honey, I can't. We can't marry now. We're too young and we have no money," Peter said.

"But I don't want you to go. I don't want to be here alone," she begged.

He hugged her and patted her shoulder in a reassuring way, although her words spooked him for some reason. He couldn't put his finger on exactly why he had such a bad feeling, but those parting words rang in his ears for months and years to come.

*   *   *

Nana appeared elated the day Peter left . . . she giggled and talked about the most inane things. In order to ease Elise's grief, she offered a shopping trip to Rich's department store. Her excitement over Elise's pending departure for Athens, some fifty miles away, dominated their conversation. Nana appeared to be more excited than sad about Elise's first experience of living away from home.

"I'm looking forward to it and scared, all in one," Elise said. "And I know I'll miss Claudie's fried chicken and her keeping my room so clean and neat."

Nana and Pops had brought Claudie with them when they moved from West End to Ansley Park.

Having Claudie's help in the household enabled Nana to sew, read, or spend time with Elise, and the pair toured gardens, visited museums, or attended the theater, where Nana espoused her opinions and theories.

This left an indelible impression on the young Elise. "I used to think my mother knew everything. Even in college I hung on every word when she talked about religion and art. I really did believe that Mother knows best," Mom told me once with detectable regret in her voice.

As much as the two of them discussed life, religion and art, rarely did they talk about male/female relationships. The only time Nana broached this topic was before Elise left for college; she told her to be careful around boys. "They're old enough to think about man things," she said.

Elise arrived in Athens a week before classes started. The University of Georgia looked like a college brochure with its gently rolling hills, abundant use of Georgia marble and red brick, heavily treed walkways, and the famous entryway arch. The Athens merchants welcomed the students like honored guests.

During the summer Elise had exchanged letters with Suzy, her roommate-to-be, and she hoped they would become friends. The social activities outlined in the orientation materials, as well as Greek rush, excited her. Even Nana encouraged Elise to join a sorority. "It's what a young woman from a good family does," she said.

Suzy caught everyone's attention with her tall, slender figure, full breasts, and blonde hair. Oblivious to whistles and stares, she told Elise she just wanted to have fun. Then maybe get married.

"Mother and Daddy want me to find a good husband," Suzy said. "And the way to find a good husband is to join a sorority."

Elise knew very little about the various houses, but Suzy could recite the reputation of each of the sororities: the Kappas had brains, the Pi Phi's money, and the Tri Delt's were beauty queens. Suzy amazed Elise with her knowledge considering that both had arrived on campus at the same time.

"I've been around the block, honey," Suzy said. Elise thought she understood what that meant, but she wasn't sure. She suddenly felt naïve and unsophisticated.

One morning during the first week of classes, the roommates headed across campus. They cut through a park to save time. Suzy glanced down and pointed at a pale-colored piece of rubber. "Oh my, someone's been getting some loving," she said.

Elise looked again. "It's a balloon, isn't it?" she asked.

Suzy howled. "It's a condom."

A red-faced Elise nodded. "If you knew my mother, you'd understand why I don't know anything. In fact, you might wonder how I was even born," she said.

After the glamour of sorority rush and the amazement that both girls selected Kappa Alpha Theta, things settled down into a routine. Suzy socialized while Elise studied. She missed Peter. Occasionally, she pulled the engagement ring out from the back of her jewelry box and wore it. Suzy sighed if she caught her. "You can't marry the first guy who asks you," she said.

Suzy met Vance, head of ROTC, the first month of school. She learned that he picked the girls for homecoming court that year. He shared his idea of including a blonde, a brunette, and a redhead. "Actually, I'm thinking of you and your roommate for the blonde and the redhead. Interested?" he asked.

Elise gasped when Suzy broke the news. The girls jumped up and down with excitement and ran to their closet in search of something great to wear. Elise wondered who would be more proud, her mother or Peter. As it happened, Peter called the next day. When Elise shared the news with him, he got quiet—which confused her. Peter finally admitted he didn't want other men gawking at her. He asked her to decline.

Nana thrilled over the news, but after Elise shared what Peter had said, she angered.

"Elise, you are a beautiful girl, and I am proud to know you've been asked to be in the festivities. I think Peter's opinion points out his jealousy," Nana said.

Suzy sided with Nana. She pleaded with Elise to be a part of the court and not tell Peter. Elise considered doing so, but in the end she withdrew.

On homecoming day, Elise sat in the stands with her other sorority sisters as Suzy and the rest of the court passed by in decorated convertibles. The band played while fans cheered. Several guys whistled and chanted. Elise suddenly felt hemmed in and angry for letting Peter tell her what to do. She left early.

In no time at all, Christmas vacation beckoned. Elise loved Christmas, something that became clearer to her once she left home. For the first time, she hadn't been able to help Nana decorate the tree and the house. Each year before that, the two spent days constructing a wreath for the front door, stringing several dozen lights around the pine tree in the front lawn, and decorating the thick mantel over the fireplace. They trimmed the living room archways with garlands and pine cones.

Nana treasured the Christmas tree ornaments that had been collected and passed down over the years. Elise knew the story of each one by heart, so much so that when Nana would unwrap one and hold it up, Elise would answer, "Aunt Pearl's crocheted heart," or "Uncle Bipp's reindeer he made as a boy."

Sometimes one of them took a minute, completely silent, and paced the room with the object in hand as they looked at the tree and became lost in memory: both women were more sentimental than they admitted.

Elise arrived in Atlanta two days before Christmas. As much as she regretted missing the chance to decorate, when she opened the front door she found the house aglow with festive celebration. "It's never been more beautiful," she said. "I hadn't realized just how home-sick I was until now."

When Nana and Pops announced all the neighborhood and family plans for the next week, Elise listened and fidgeted. "Peter got a three day pass and he'll be here any minute," she said.

Nana coughed and stared straight ahead.

Elise ran down the steep concrete steps to the street when she heard the familiar horn beep. She couldn't wait another second to hug and kiss him. When Peter embraced her, he held on for a long time. "I missed you more than you know," he whispered as if someone might overhear.

Peter greeted Nana and Pops. Something appeared to be different. Elise hoped that maybe Nana had experienced a change of heart. Weeks before,

Kitty wrote to tell Elise about the advice she gave Nana: "You better accept Peter because Elise is going to marry him." Had Nana listened?

"Perhaps you and Peter want to invite your friends over tonight? We could roll up the rugs and y'all could dance," Nana offered.

Elise and Peter jabbed each other in disbelief. They took the gesture as a peace offering, a Christmas present in and of itself.

Jimmie and Eugenia showed up first with an armful of records. Wink, Louise, Ida and the Eatin' boys followed. The living room buzzed with laughter and music until midnight. It was just like it always had been: fun and frolic with friends.

After everyone else had left, Elise walked Peter to his car. The evening had filled them with hope and joy. "Tomorrow at ten for presents and breakfast," she said.

"Will you wear your ring tomorrow? That's all I want for Christmas," Peter said.

Elise did not sleep well that night. She tossed and turned, threw off the covers and woke up with shivers. Finally after sheer exhaustion, she dozed off.

She dreamed of a church, familiar in some ways. She watched herself get out of the family car in a wedding dress—smiling, wearing red lipstick, and carrying such an oversized bouquet of white roses that she needed both arms to carry. A groom emerged from the church to meet her. As he neared, his face came into focus. She dropped the flowers. It wasn't Peter.

The next morning everyone took turns and opened gifts. Pops and Peter both got handkerchiefs and fountain pens. They laughed about it. When the fun died down, Peter produced a box with a giant green bow and held it out to Elise.

"I love presents," she giggled. "Especially a big one that has my name on it."

She ripped the bow off. The box dropped away as she lifted out a blue damask bathrobe. "It's beautiful," she sighed.

Nana gasped. "This is not appropriate. Much too intimate of a gift. You'll have to take it back, Peter."

"Ma'am, I meant for her to have it for school. No other reason," he said.

Nana left the room.

*   *   *

Elise and Peter continued to write into the spring of 1942. Each prayed for Nana to change her mind or give up out of fatigue. The couple convinced each other that nothing could keep them apart.

Four months after the strained Christmas vacation, Peter planned to be in Atlanta on leave, but he had to cancel at the last minute. Elise and the old gang decided to get together. They stayed out late dancing and talking.

On Saturday morning, Elise passed through the dining room. The table was partially set with a linen tablecloth and the good china. "What's this, Mother?" she asked.

Nana announced that she had signed up with the Red Cross to have navy men over for Sunday dinner. "Pilots," Nana said. "Yankee pilots."

Elise nodded dutifully. "The table looks lovely. I'd say the men are in for true Southern hospitality."

Nana ignored the remark. She skirted around Elise to the window and pulled it open. A slight breeze puffed out the sheer curtains and started a wave at the bottom of the tablecloth. "There'll be two of them. Maybe you could invite your friend, Emma?"

Part III

Ohio and Atlanta, early 1960s

Mom started her ninth year as a part-time college student at Baldwin Wallace College as my high school graduation neared. The temporary teacher's certificate she had received when she started teaching did not stipulate a degree completion date, as long as she continued to take appropriate courses toward her degree. When she had transferred her credits from University of Georgia, almost a years' worth of credits were disallowed—which meant she still needed to complete two years of basic liberal arts courses plus the requirements for a degree in education. During her second summer at Baldwin Wallace Mom met Vennetta, who was also teaching with a temporary certificate under the same conditions as Mom. After striking up a friendship, the pair car-pooled to campus each summer. Vennetta didn't look younger than Mom—other than she had a beautiful face and violet eyes. Her solid, tall frame fit the image of a farmer's wife, but Vennetta shared Mom's dislike of cattle and manure.

Once in a while, I rode with them and poked around downtown Berea while they were in class. Afterward the three of us sometimes lunched or visited an interesting store.

I teased Mom about the *years* it was taking her to finish. "You and I might end up with our college degrees at the same time," I said. We all laughed, but Vennetta defended her.

"Just remember you've got it easy, Nancy. You don't have to raise three kids and take care of a husband," she said.

Even though they both juggled many responsibilities, I rarely heard either of them complain about the added burdens of studying or attending summer courses. They both seemed invigorated by the professors and their assignments. My curiosity was piqued, too, so much that Mom once got permission from her professor to let me sit in. The kind instructor included me in his question-and-answer period, which got me even more excited for college. I had lost interest in high school—I viewed it as cliquish, probably because I wasn't part of the *in* crowd. Over the years, I'd drifted apart from Marilyn and Betty, my best friends from first grade. The three of us had been inseparable until junior high, when Betty moved to Medina, and Marilyn, matured into a beautiful girl who moved into the top tier of popular kids. She didn't abandon me, but I felt left out. Neither invited to the best parties, nor on the varsity cheerleading squad, I formed new friends the last two years in high school. I eagerly anticipated college, which I considered a promotion in life.

As university life loomed, I loved listening to Mom or Vennetta reminisce about their own early college days and how different things had been when they were coeds. Mom must have told Vennetta things about Peter because every once in a while one of them used his name, as if they forgot I was there. Then they would quickly change the subject.

"He used to call her every year on her birthday," I once offered, to prove I knew something of the guy. I wanted them to keep talking so I'd learn more. Vennetta smiled at my remark but didn't say a word.

"When was the last time he called, Mom?" I pressed. She flustered. Vennetta perked up as if she wanted to hear the answer. Even when you sensed her interest, she never probed.

"I think just before my fortieth," Mom said.

The idea of multiple boyfriends must have been hard for Vennetta to grasp. From what I'd seen she seemed ill at ease around men in general, and she was not even that comfortable around her own husband, Elmer. Plus, Vennetta's athletic and big-boned frame wasn't the picture of a girl guys rushed to date. Despite her porcelain skin, she didn't possess much feminine charm.

Vennetta and Elmer lived five miles from us. Although their farm was roughly the same size as ours, they seemed to make more money—mainly because Elmer had diversified into buying and selling land and started a lucrative trucking business. "Everything the man touches turns to gold," Vennetta once remarked.

Given Vennetta's independence, our family speculated that she taught school in order to do something for herself, not because of finances. And she probably wanted her own money. Elmer struck me as the kind who required an accounting of every penny.

Mom and Vennetta bonded over their love of exploring: they attended concerts, plays, and museums in Cleveland, or took boat rides on Lake Erie. They both relished having a like-minded companion, since neither Dad nor Elmer longed for adventure. Elmer liked to watch television or meet his friends in bars, while Dad simply wanted to be home.

Mom's friendship with Helen also grew. Helen was an activist before the word gained respect. Although the two women approached injustice differently, they agreed in principle. Mom admired Helen's spunk and intelligence. Helen had been widowed in her forties, and despite debilitating arthritis and an average appearance, she never wanted for male companionship. Helen loved divulging details about her partners and offering humorous observations about men.

"Fascinating creatures," she often said. "I can't decide if they are more boy or horn dog."

Mom introduced Vennetta to Helen and they hit if off. As much as they tried to plan events for the three of them, it happened infrequently due to Helen's many interests and her long list of friends.

If I appeared unexpectedly during one of the trio's get-togethers, I usually found them in raucous laughter that went unexplained. These conversations illuminated different aspects of their personalities, however. For example, Vennetta's face reddened at the slightest suggestive remark, which made Mom seem progressive. Even though Mom proclaimed naivety, she had a completely open mind about sex. Apparently, Mom and Helen shared similar views and sex was one of their favorite topics. Eventually, they even got Vennetta to open up and discuss the subject more freely.

Alta also remained a steady friend of my Mom's and a fixture at the farm. Unlike others who called before visiting, she usually popped in on her way home from her clerical job in Medina. Sometimes she stayed for coffee or dinner, if her son was staying overnight with a friend. Her visits were so frequent we didn't consider her "company." She liked to laugh and Dad always thought of something to kid her about . . . how she parked her car, her hairdo, or if she wanted to help us bale hay on the weekend.

Alta was the youngest of Mom's friends and the most fragile: petite, fine features, thinning hair, pale skin and so prone to colds that she never seemed completely healthy. Alta's husband died during WW II, leaving her a widow at twenty-two. Along with forthrightness, Alta wore her heart on her sleeve. Once, when I was fourteen, I walked into the living room to find Alta sobbing in Mom's arms. I excused myself, embarrassed to have interrupted. Only much later did Mom tell what upset Alta that day: she missed sex and didn't know if she'd ever have it again.

"I feel so alone and old," she said.

"Nonsense. You're only thirty-six," Mom said.

A pep talk ensued and Dad added finding a boyfriend for Alta to his list of teases. As tacky as that sounds, he always made people laugh and feel better.

The tight bond between Mom and her friends flourished over the years through acceptance and respect for their differences—namely their upbringing and family experiences.

Unlike Elise, who had Nana's companionship throughout her childhood and early adult years, Vennetta's mother had died when she was five years old. Afterward, her playboy father separated Vennetta from her sister and shipped each one off to live with a different aunt, so he could pursue women without the worry of raising children. After several years and at wife number three's insistence, he reunited the sisters and brought them back to live with him and his wife in Cleveland. The wife gave Vennetta the only kindness and mothering she ever knew. Unfortunately, the playboy discarded wife number three.

"Dad enjoyed the chase," Vennetta said once. "As soon as he married a woman, he'd be out looking for the next one."

I weighed that remark. "How many wives did he have?" I asked.

When she answered "eight" my mouth fell open. "How could he afford all that alimony?"

She didn't hesitate. "He made their lives so miserable that they felt grateful just to get away from him. He never gave any of them a penny."

When it came to pressing Vennetta about her past, Mom controlled her curiosity more than I did. She never asked questions. Instead, she waited for Vennetta to offer information. I, however, plowed right ahead. I couldn't fathom such a father. His antics sounded like something out of a movie. I asked Vennetta if I could meet him. For once, Mom joined in, "I'd like to meet him, too."

Vennetta often dropped by the farm during Nana's yearly visits. Having grown up without a mother, Mom and Nana's relationship intrigued her. Vennetta also seemed to sense a kindred spirit in Nana, since they shared similar straight-laced views of life. Plus, Nana was a skillful storyteller if she felt comfortable with a person. She shared stories with Vennetta that I'd heard before, but she told them in a new way. I especially loved all the tales about Margaret Mitchell, author of *Gone with the Wind*, who had lived down the street during Mom's childhood. According to Nana, Margaret based Rhett Butler on her own handsome rogue of a husband named Red. Nana said the two had a stormy and short-lived marriage, but that they still *met up* from time to time—which was considered quite scandalous in conservative Atlanta society.

"Margaret had a bit of Scarlet in her, completely nonplussed over what society made of her actions," Nana said.

Vennetta borrowed Mom's copy of the book after one such afternoon of sipping iced tea and spinning yarns.

Even though Mom had taught for six years, Nana still made her objections known, without ever asking *why* Mom worked. Mom shared her frustration and disappointment with Vennetta, who listened intently.

"She's concerned about you," Vennetta pointed out. "My Dad only said I didn't have the brains to ever make it through college." The remark overwhelmed Mom with sadness, but before she could express sympathy, Vennetta laughed and continued, "I showed him though—graduated early with honors."

While that perspective softened Mom's resentment of Nana's criticisms, Vennetta charmed Nana. A new giggle streak emerged from Nana, who delighted in having a new audience to share her family memories with. After one such afternoon she invited Vennetta to Atlanta. Nana suggested that Vennetta be included in Mom's next visit: we kids had already stopped going on the annual trip South.

Nana offered that Aunt Kitty had plenty of room in her house given that all of her children were out on their own.

"Kitty and I both love an excuse to show off our city," Nana said.

Vennetta accepted on the spot, delighted at the offer. Mom decided that taking both Vennetta and Alta might be fun. When Aunt Kitty concurred, the eager threesome made plans.

"Wait until you see the house," Alta said to Vennetta. "And wait 'til you meet Mat. She'll spoil us rotten."

The girls' road trip down to Georgia in 1961 created opportunity for laughter and conversation. Mom and Vennetta shared the task of driving. The advent of multiple freeways made the trip less painful than it had been that first drive down years earlier with us three kids.

Alta told stories from the backseat about things she and Mom had done on previous trips, which increased Vennetta's anticipation all the more.

"Cocktail hour with Harllee presiding is always a highlight," Alta chuckled. "And if Elise isn't tired of Aunt Fanny's cabin, we should go there for fried chicken. It's a tourist trap but lots of fun."

Each story increased the excitement. Out of nowhere, Alta laughed heartily.

"Elise, did you ever tell Vennetta about Sylvia?" Alta asked.

Mom shook her head, and Vennetta turned around in the passenger seat to give Alta her full attention.

Alta took a big breath. "Well, Kitty took Elise and me to her book club meeting as guests. Before things started a rather snooty-looking woman, Sylvia, discovered we lived in Ohio and questioned us at length about many things. But the topper was when she wanted to know what our club was like. Elise and I puzzled over that and said that we read every chance we got but we didn't have a book club. 'No, no . . . I mean country club.' When we told her Lodi didn't have that kind of club either, she gasped. She said she could never live in a place that didn't have a country club."

Vennetta roared.

"So now whenever Elise and I drive through a new little town one of us usually says, "Wonder if they have a club here?"

All the excited chatter made the two day drive go quickly; soon Mom turned off Nancy Creek Road onto Kitty's driveway. She honked all the way up the hill, as she always had done.

"Can you believe this place, Vennetta?" Alta said, leaning over the front seat like a little kid wanting attention.

Each time Mom visited Kitty's house, it seemed more splendid. The azaleas more lush amid taller dogwoods and pines and from the bottom of the ultra-steep driveway, the sprawling two-story Georgian colonial looked like it would drop off the top of the hill. A larger white brick center dominated equally large wings on either side. Dark shutters framed all of the windows—completing the look of understated elegance.

"Oh my," Vennetta said.

After warm welcomes from Kitty, the three visitors lounged on the screened-in porch. Mat poured iced teas and offered them small sandwiches, knowing they would have been hungry after their long journey. Afterward, Kitty toured them through her gardens and later drove them around some of the more picturesque residential areas. Everyone relaxed in the comfortable surroundings and Southern hospitality.

The next day everyone except Mom disappeared for an afternoon nap. Mom leafed through a *Saturday Evening Post*. Suddenly she had a strong urge to see Peter, or at least talk to him on the phone. Maybe because she was there without children, she let herself imagine what it would be like to hear his voice or see his face.

She stepped into Harllee's library and closed the door. She remembered Peter's office number he had given to her once when he called. She had never used it. Her heart pounded as she dialed the number.

Peter answered on the second ring. Her voice surprised and thrilled him. When she quickly added that she was at Kitty's, he said he'd be right over.

"Oh, no. Don't do that," she said.

"Elise, I have to see you."

Mom suggested they "accidentally" run into each other at the shopping center on Paces Ferry and Northside Road. They planned to meet in an hour.

At the last minute, Mom worried about her plan. When Alta woke up from her nap, she invited her to go, perhaps as a sort of chaperone. Mom admitted to me years later how nervous she had been.

"My stomach churned and my mouth was dry. We hadn't seen each other for eight years," she said and then added, "It was Pop's funeral, and I went alone since your dad had to stay at the farm."

Peter had brought his wife, Vivian, to pay respects to Pops. The three of them talked briefly after the service—cordial but short. Mom watched Peter and his wife walk away from the church: she said they looked good together and it made her jealous.

On the way to the shopping center Mom recalled the event and pondered what Peter would look like. A lot of things can change in eight years.

After Mom parked the car, she and Alta headed toward the shops.

Peter spotted her right away. He got out of his Buick and called out, "Hey! Elise."

"Oh, my goodness. Peter," Mom said, smiling and giving what Alta deemed an Oscar-winning performance.

Quick introductions led to stalled conversation. Mom couldn't think of a thing to say—she just wanted to stare at him. His clothes were fashionable, he still looked fairly fit and his hair thick as ever, with only a hint of gray. Alta gave him the once-over. In fact, she seemed the only one at ease.

"Are you married?" Alta finally asked with a bit of a smirk.

Undaunted, Peter answered yes and turned to Mom. "And how is Richard?"

Mom later said both she and Peter were uncomfortable. To end the awkwardness they said their good-byes.

Once Peter walked out of earshot, Alta locked arms with Mom. "So Peter . . . the one you were engaged to, right?"

Mom nodded.

Alta paused. "Must have been a hard decision."

Mom said the bittersweet reunion confused her. She thought about Peter for the rest of the trip and all the way back to Ohio. Within days of her return to the farm, however, she let it go.

From my earliest memory, Mom and Dad talked about me going to college, and I never questioned it. I think I assumed that when the time came, I'd simply pick the school I wanted and go there. I didn't consider that my inconsistent grades or poor SAT scores might complicate matters. My lackadaisical attitude toward my studies apparently mirrored Dad. I picked Muskingum College in Ohio, but they refused me. Dad told me he hadn't paid much attention to his studies in high school either and had been forced to repeat some courses after graduation in order to get into college. Thankfully, my situation wasn't that dire, but disappointment overwhelmed me. Clearly, I had done too little, too late.

Lilly jumped in with a solution. After some research she found Hillsdale College, one state north. "It's like an Ivy League school, only in Michigan," she promised as I scowled. "Lots of kids from Shaker Heights go there. And you know that is the best neighborhood in all of Cleveland."

The only thing Dad liked about the idea was the school's size of nine hundred students, and that they eventually accepted me. I tried to feel excited about going to a college no one had ever heard of.

To celebrate my acceptance to Hillsdale, Mom and I drove to Cleveland for a major shopping trip to Higbee's department store. Even though the heat of summer persisted, the back-to-school fall line-ups of wool plaids and cardigans were everywhere. We rode the escalator to the fifth floor, where I made a beeline for the Bobby Brooks and Villager racks. I selected skirts, kilts, and blouses with roll-up sleeves and headed for the dressing room. Usually the attentive shopper, Mom seemed to be elsewhere—apathetic even.

"The best years of your life. You'll like college, Nance," she said wistfully. "Sure will be different not hearing your laugh. Your brother's going to miss you."

I didn't really digest what she said, since I had immersed myself in wanting all the clothes I tried on and already pictured myself strolling Hillsdale's campus in my new outfits. As we approached the check-out counter, I noticed a corduroy jacket on a mannequin. I immediately remembered the brown, full-length corduroy coat with a fox-trimmed hood that Mom had bought me on my sixteenth birthday. "Look, Mom," I pointed.

She smiled and nodded. "Nothing as special as yours. I still love you in that coat."

I hugged her. "You know what I remember about that day?" She frowned and shook her head. "You put a new dress for yourself back on the rack in order to buy that coat for me."

She claimed not to remember, but I doubted it. More likely she just downplayed a generous gesture.

"You were so unselfish. It made me feel bad . . . for a little while," I said.

Her moist eyes suddenly dried as she burst out laughing.

We wound our way out of Cleveland and back to the farm. Mom drove the new Oldsmobile that Dad had bought earlier that year, a step up for our family. Its shiny black exterior and red leather interior made it the flashiest car we'd ever owned. I rubbed my hand over the seat, still in disbelief that Dad bought it.

"Now that Dad has his airplane and motorcycle, maybe he'll start buying more nice things like this for you," I said.

She smiled but said nothing. If she ever wanted for material goods, I sure never saw any evidence of it.

"I can't believe all of you are growing up so fast. I'd like to go back eight years and have that as a present," she said, sighing. "Those were my happiest times."

Her confession shocked me. My memories of eight years prior meant hardship: tons of farm work, a house in disarray as we slowly remodeled it, an upstairs that was colder than a snow cone, and the discomfort of riding in the old Ford truck's open-air bed in little wooden chairs Dad made for us, before Pops gave us the Nash.

"You're kidding. It was awful," I said. I started to remind her of my version of the past. She stopped me.

"But somewhere in there, after all the hard work, I knew we would make it. All of our efforts paid off. All of you were good kids. It's my best memory," she said.

She looked straight ahead and concentrated on Route 42. Even though she drove better than her friend Alta, she never had been an especially skilled driver. Her hand wiped away a tear.

I watched her for a bit and wondered, "You weren't sorry about the choice you made? Leaving Atlanta and ending up on a farm? C'mon."

A car whizzed past us and honked. Her slow driving slowed even more.

"I loved your dad. Still do. And yes, I miss Atlanta. But Ohio is my home." She abruptly concentrated on tuning the radio to a station I hated. I groaned. More Lawrence Welk music.

That summer, Dad built three stalls in the barn. The first one had heavy timbered gates, high walls and thick metal latches. I couldn't imagine what in the heck he planned to put in there. Nobody said a word, least of all Mom since she hadn't been in the barn in years. Richie finally tripped up and said something about a Percheron.

"Those monsters that pull beer wagons?" I asked.

"No, those are Clydesdales," Richie explained. "But Percherons are similar. Both are draft horses."

I wondered why or how Dad became interested in them.

"Do we ride them? Not that *I* would," I said.

Richie said Dad wanted to raise them. Maybe show them so he could establish a name as a breeder. It sounded crazy. More work!

"Mom doesn't know yet," Richie said in a hushed voice.

Soon enough, the whole family knew of Dad's latest endeavor. The first giant of a horse arrived, and it was not that tame. Richie and Sally, unfazed by its size, took up leading it around. They told me repeatedly how gentle she was. I couldn't see past the enormous feet, and I imagined one of us with broken bones if the horse stepped in the wrong direction. Dad helped Sally onto the lofty perch one day, and she screamed with joy as the horse galloped away with her. It made my stomach roll just to watch. Mom stood beside me and shook her head.

"Oh my," she said. I nudged her and whispered that I couldn't have said it better myself.

"There are three pens out in barn. Did you know?" I said.

She surprised me by nodding agreement. Her shoulders shrugged in a defeated motion. "I want Rich to be happy. But he sure does make more work for himself."

Dad spent every spare minute with the horse. He groomed her, led her around by the halter, worked on commands, and let the horse get accustomed to him. He said trust between the two was key, and everything went smoothly for weeks.

One Saturday Mom changed bedsheets while the three of us watched a western on television. All of the sudden the backdoor flew open and there was a huge crash in the kitchen, followed by a garbled moan. Richie rushed in first, with Sally and me close behind. Dad lay on the linoleum floor up against the refrigerator. Blood oozed from the side of his head. His hand covered his mouth. By then Mom had appeared with a towel and knelt beside him. She began to cry. "What happened? We need to get to the hospital."

Dad spit into the towel. Several teeth and bloody mucus fell out. A rancid whiff churned my stomach as I stood paralyzed.

Richie caught Mom as she slumped over. Dad motioned for Richie to get water. Mom swayed but didn't lose consciousness. I gathered her up and tried not to look at Dad.

Richie dabbed at the hole in Dad's scalp. By then Mom composed herself and took over.

Dad opened his mouth a bit. "Ouch. Damn it. Hurts."

"What happened?" Mom asked.

"The horse kicked me. My fault. Got in the wrong place. Now I'll really need to get the rest of my teeth pulled," Dad said.

Mom used to repeat how much she noticed Dad's teeth when they first met. "So straight and white," she'd say.

I guess they were straight and white but I don't remember wonderful—only how often Dad visited our dentist, Dr. Fry. His soft teeth decayed at a record pace. After one too many lectures, Dad decided not to delay the inevitable. "Pull em all, doc." Dr. Fry laughed but didn't obey.

Up until then, Mom had objected every time Dad brought it up. She insisted he was too young to have false teeth. But after the damage that day Dad finally got his wish. At age forty-four, all of his teeth were removed. He aged instantly. His resulting misshapen jaw and strange voice freaked us out.

Mom tried not to notice, but it was too much, even for her. A few weeks after the accident, I had joined my parents in the kitchen for some tea.

"How long will it be until you get your teeth?" she asked Dad.

"Two months. Dr. Fry wants the gums completely healed."

Mom paled. She hated the news, I could tell. I didn't like how he looked either, but I kept it to myself.

Dad reached over and patted her hand. "I told Fry to make my new teeth even whiter and prettier," he said, like a junior high boy who'd just passed his first love note.

I hesitated. "But Dad, you'll have your new teeth when you and Mom take me to Hillsdale. Right?"

Dad tried to sip his tea. "Don't worry. I won't embarrass you."

Later that summer, two more horses arrived, but I paid little attention. I counted the days until I'd leave for college. I tried on all my new outfits, again and again. Letters arrived from my roommates: Mary from Indiana and Blair from Michigan. They teased me about being a farm girl, since neither of them had any friends who lived in the country. This worried me briefly—I hadn't considered that I might be viewed as different. Farms were common in my high school. Somehow, I dismissed it. There were too many reasons for celebration: no more chores, no more manure, and no more concern about whether my hair stunk from silage. Merely studying and having fun would be a snap!

As the day approached for me to leave for Hillsdale, Dad told Mom he wanted to "have a talk" with me before I left. She delivered the message.

"What about?" I asked her, puzzled.

She giggled. "He's been preparing for a week. I'd like to hear it myself."

Later that evening, I met Dad on the front porch. He smiled like his old self—he had finally received, and adjusted to, the new dentures. He sat in our big wicker chair with stacks of books at his feet. I had never seen him more nervous.

"Mom said you wanted to talk to me," I started.

He flushed. "We're proud of you, string bean. Don't forget who you are."

I nodded.

"Is there anything you want to know? About boys? Sex?" He talked so fast I almost missed it. It was all I could do to stifle a laugh.

"It's kind of late for that, don't you think?" I said. "I mean, I have had boyfriends: Greg, Jim, and of course, Dave."

He frowned. I quickly realized my blunder.

"Mom and I have talked, you know, about all of that."

He relaxed and pointed to the books. "Well, if you need it, I have information."

The night before I left for school, I ambled out to the old barn and sat down on the concrete ramp. I took in the view of the corn crib where Richie and I had formed our "secret" headquarters as kids, of the corral where Dad worked with the horses, and of the apple orchard where Richie and I tried to camp out once (before I got scared and retreated back to the house). The white wooden fencing surrounding the corral, reminiscent of Kentucky farms, was one of the first improvements Dad finished. He'd said it gave the farm a statement when people drove in. I smiled as I remembered how Richie and I challenged each other to see who could walk farther across the fence top before falling. We pretended to be tightrope walkers as we balanced on its two inches of width, one foot in front of another, taking a breather on the larger posts every ten feet.

The farm had been my home for twelve years. I walked around and recalled the fun, the injuries, the hours we spent on our make shift basketball court, and all the times Richie and I tramped out to the end of the fields to bring the cows in for milking. It didn't feel sad—it felt like a right of passage.

Mom and Dad helped me pack the Olds for the trip to Hillsdale. As we headed out the driveway, Richie appeared out of nowhere and waved awkwardly without a smile. That put a lump in my throat. Mom noticed but didn't say a word.

Mom and Dad exchanged stories and memories on the five-hour drive to the campus. Every once in a while, Dad pointed out a barn he thought considered special. He quizzed Mom as we passed a field.

"What kind of cows are those, El?"

"Brown ones," she replied, even though she had learned the difference between a Jersey and a Guernsey cow years before. She always gave the same answer, and he always laughed. I shook my head at the two of them, stuck on the same old joke.

"I have some news, Nancy." Mom turned from the front seat and patted my knee. "It appears I'm going to get my college degree this year."

Dad eyed me in the rearview mirror. "Your mother petitioned the dean of education department. Nobody messes with this redhead!" I leaned forward to hear the story.

Mom said the college had periodically changed graduation requirements from the time she started nine years earlier.

"So unfair," she explained. "I had nearly twice the credits I needed with no end in sight. The dean agreed with me and gave me his assurance in writing that after the next two courses I will graduate."

"Good for you, Mom," I said, and I meant it. "It's been a long ordeal. Most people would have quit."

The trip was uneventful, except that my chronic car sickness forced me to move up to the front seat between Mom and Dad. As we neared the campus, Mom put her arm up behind me on the back of the seat. "I hope no one sees us," I mumbled. "It'll look like you don't want to let go of your little girl."

The inviting, shaded streets in the small town of Hillsdale calmed my nerves. How could anything that looked like it belonged on a church calendar be intimidating?

I leaned forward to steal a glimpse of Dad and double-check his dentures. He caught me and shook his head. He smiled weird and crossed his eyes. "I look fine. My teeth are straighter than yours, kiddo."

Big posters with arrows pointed the way toward registration. I tried to recall the names of the modern dorms, hoping that one of those would be my new home with Mary and Blair. After check-in, we drove to Mauck Hall, one of the *oldest* dorms on campus. Yet there was something stately about the red brick, heavy columns, and leaded-glass front doors. I assured myself that it would be fine.

We climbed the stairs to Room 310, where Mary and Blair, each with their parents in tow unpacked amid utter chaos. Too many people had squeezed into a room barely large enough for one person. All the parents eventually excused themselves as we hugged one another and fell into rushed conversation about the dorm mother, our schedules, who wanted what bed, and where in the heck we could put all of our clothes. A carton of Salem cigarettes fell out of Mary's suitcase as we jostled luggage. Blair shrugged and I gasped.

"You smoke cigarettes? Is that allowed?" I blurted. They cracked up.

"Should be an interesting year," Blair kidded.

The majority of Hillsdale college students came from wealthy families. Student conversations centered on clothes, fancy cars, what camps they had attended, what foreign countries they had visited, or where their family might vacation for Christmas.

Though Blair's family was affluent (her father a doctor), she made no distinction about who had what or where they'd grown up—which made her an exception to the majority of girls I would meet at Hillsdale. After I got to know her parents I understood why Blair was so unassuming. They were friendly and comfortable. Whenever they visited Blair, they included Mary and me in their dinner plans. "C'mon girls, my treat," Dr. Bullard would say.

Hillsdale had a beautiful campus in 1963. The entire grounds took up one square block, with fraternity and sorority houses lining the perimeter. The cafeteria rivaled the food at any fine restaurant, and the contemporary library had more books than you'd ever expect for the size of the college. Most of my classes had no more than fifteen students. However, the comfortable environment for learning felt smaller than high school.

After Greek Week ended, Blair, Mary, and I ended up in three different sororities and spent less time together. I liked a few girls in my pledge class, though, and started to feel connected to the sorority and the college.

I yearned for home sometimes, too. Phone calls to Ohio were too expensive for my budget. But after a month or so I relented and called collect. Mom answered. Her accent shocked me—with time and distance, I heard just how much of a drawl she had. I kidded her about whether she'd been practicing. Dad used to say her accent improved after each trip to Georgia.

"How's it going, darlin'?" she said.

I felt tears coming but stopped myself. I wanted support, not help or sympathy. We made small talk. Eventually, I told her how wealthy most of the kids were and how out of place I felt. She sloughed it off. "There will always be someone with more money, no matter how much you have," she said and then changed the subject.

Her common sense lifted my spirit. I knew money wasn't the most important thing, yet I wanted some—I always had. But sharing that news with her wouldn't be in my best interest. Nor should I divulge my desire to leave Hillsdale. Before I could say anything else, Mom made a revelation of her own.

"I've caused a stir at school," she said in a boastful way. "Remember how I complained about our incompetent principal, Sam?"

She told me how she and Helen organized the teachers and filed a complaint to Mr. White, the county superintendent. The complaint cited, among other irregularities, how Sam listened in on the teachers using the PA system. As a retired drill sergeant, he regularly inspected coat rooms for neatness and wrote out demerits to wayward teachers. Mom called him a sneaky boar.

Apparently, Mr. White thought the teachers should have first confronted Sam directly instead of filing a complaint. He organized a mandatory meeting for everyone to attend.

"Who would like to speak to Sam face to face and voice your concern?" Mr. White said to kick off the discussion.

Mom said she stood right up, looked Sam in the eye, and started through her list of complaints. Helen joined in. I pictured the two of them giving Sam an earful. I grinned at the very thought. Working seemed to have brought out some kind of rebel or strength in Mom. She no longer tolerated wrong doings.

"So guess what happened last week?" she asked without waiting for me to answer. "Someone gave Mr. White a tip that Sam stole four hundred dollars from the school coffers and hid it in his trunk. They just arrested him. Can you believe it?"

I had wanted to talk about my problems, but hearing about Mom's small victory diverted my thoughts and helped more than she knew.

I studied all the time. If I got good grades I'd be able to transfer to a school I liked. Miami University, Ohio (which was bigger) and Ohio State (the biggest) piqued my interest. Either choice would be five hundred dollars a year less than Hillsdale, which I planned to use as a selling point with Dad. Unfortunately, Dad felt comfortable with me at Hillsdale, because he perceived it as safe and sheltered.

John Kennedy's assassination happened that November. We students huddled around the sole television in the dorm living room muffling sobs and sharing our grief with one another. The young president had renewed our spirit and pride in the United States. Who could have committed such an atrocity? People cried for the loss of life and hope. Classes were cancelled, and within hours the campus was closed, as were most others across the country. Everyone left early for Thanksgiving vacation, not that it felt like a holiday or a vacation.

Dad cried openly during the televised funeral. When John-John saluted his father's casket as it passed in front of him, Dad left the room. No one spoke. Mom followed Dad up the stairs. It scared us to see Dad cry like that. Sally disappeared to her room while Richie and I headed for the barn.

Once back at Hillsdale, I continued to study and eventually dated. It made me like the college better but not enough. As Christmas approached, Blair invited me to spend the break at her house.

"We have a ski vacation planned to Boyne Mountain in northern Michigan. My parents would love to have you join us," she said.

It sounded like fun but I knew I didn't have money for that kind of thing . . . and I didn't want to admit it. She must have figured it out.

"Listen, it won't cost you anything. Dad said to be sure and tell you that you're our guest," Blair said.

We started planning. It would be my first holiday without my parents, and it promised excitement. I felt as special as the kid from my high school whose parents had taken him to Hawaii for graduation. You had to be rich to have trips like that.

Blair's Mom picked us up from our dorm in the family station wagon. Her warm and friendly demeanor was the same as the first day I met her. She chatted about relatives and ongoing projects to their house in Clarkston,

Michigan. Blair had told me earlier that her parents had built a new home on a lake and they were still decorating it.

My eyes widened as we approached the driveway. The sleek and sprawling ranch-style house had contemporary lines and several kinds of stone. The inside resembled the "house of the future" I had seen at Disneyland. There were built-in appliances and other modern conveniences, high ceilings, and plush wall-to-wall carpeting. Oversized leather furniture dominated the house and the dining room table seated ten. The only out-of-place fixture was a huge electric organ, which Blair's dad usually played like Victor Borge at the piano: he messed around to be funny. But if he wanted to, he could really play.

The ski trip educated me on how the other half lived. We ate every meal in a restaurant. The lift tickets cost a small fortune, which Blair's family generously covered. Plus, the doctor decided I should have a new ski outfit. Maybe he felt sorry for me wearing Blair's hand-me-downs, but I bet it was just more of his generosity showing.

At the end of the week, we returned to the house in Clarkston and rested for two days before going back to Hillsdale. I tossed and turned in the extra bed in Blair's room and tried to sleep. Blair snored lightly, just like she did at school. My initial awe and pangs of jealousy at her lifestyle were replaced with waves of homesickness. Tears dampened my pillow. I wondered what Richie was up to, if Mom had made fried chicken on Sunday and what kind of progress Dad had made with those horses. I knew that Mom wouldn't have been overly impressed with the Bullard's material success, but I wondered what Dad would make of it all.

*　　*　　*

Tulips threatened to break through dormant flowerbeds in late March. It was the annual promise that the long winter in the Midwest would end. On the first warm day people broke out madras Bermuda shorts and T-shirts and tossed Frisbees out on the dorm's lawn. We skipped class. Everyone talked about going to Ft. Lauderdale for spring break. Amidst all the talk of tans, boys, and the beach, I yearned for home. It had been four months since I'd seen my family.

The week before spring break, Mom phoned to tell me Dad was in the hospital.

"Nothing serious. They're doing tests."

My mind raced with fear. My head throbbed. "What kind of tests? Dad is stronger than an ox."

Mom paused, carefully choosing her words. "The doctors think he may have had a mild heart attack. They want to observe him for a few days."

I felt sick to my stomach. Years before, Dad got the flu, and I remembered how he had still milked the cows every morning and night, like always, and then gone back to bed. He trudged on while ill for three days.

"Nancy, he had a tightness in his chest and a pain in his arm that wouldn't go away. He didn't have a blackout or anything. He's in good spirits. Teasing the nurses and such," Mom said.

I twisted the phone cord around my index finger. "Is he scared?"

"Your father?" Mom laughed. "He drove himself to the hospital and then called me to let me know where he was. Doesn't that sound like him?"

Mom assured me he would be fine. She diagnosed heart burn or some other strange, one-time malady.

"Give him my best," I said. "Call if anything changes."

Two days later, I returned to the dorm after class to find a scribbled note on my bed: "Call home right away."

Each floor of the dorm had a phone booth in the hall. My legs wobbled as I stumbled toward the phone. My hand shook as I dialed the operator and placed a collect call. The phone rang several times before Mom answered breathless and accepted the charges.

"Mom," I whispered and started to cry.

She muffled a cry. "Your dad had a massive heart attack early this morning, in the hospital. He's in and out of consciousness."

I leaned my head against the wall and held the receiver, unable to speak.

Mom blew her nose and breathed in deep. "The doctor is puzzled. Worried really, I can tell. Richie won't talk to me, and Sally has gone to pieces. I need you, we all need you."

"I'll get there as fast as I can. I promise," I said.

Mom picked me up from the bus stop and we drove straight to Lodi Hospital. Inside, we rounded the corner to the closed double doors of the intensive care unit, and I suddenly froze. The memory of my childhood tonsillectomy paralyzed me. I smelled a strong alcohol odor, along with the stench of sickness, just like before. Mom took me by the hand.

"Don't be scared. They can help him. Dr. Glosh is as good as they come," she said.

Dad lay alone in the stark white room. His six-foot frame was dwarfed by the clear plastic oxygen tent. His forearms extended out from the bottom of the tent, attached to machines. His gray skin and closed eyes made the scene unbearable. I gasped. Tears fell faster than I could wipe them away.

"Dad," I whispered as I stroked his hand. "Can you hear me?"

His hand felt lifeless. Unfamiliar. Bags of fluid, suspended from above, surrounded the bed. Needles and tubes punctured both his arms. A heart monitor beeped. The tent swelled with a "swoosh" pumping noise and then lessened. A mechanical world kept him alive.

Mom and I stood speechless for several minutes. I felt faint. Neither of us noticed Dad wake up.

"What are you doing here, string bean?" Dad said, barely audible.

I squeezed his hand. "Dad, hi. Are you okay? You look scary this way."

"You should see it from this side," he said and tried to smile.

Mom helped him with a drink of water. Pat, the head nurse, strolled into the room. Her booming voice matched her stature. "Good, you're awake. How's my favorite patient?"

"Bet you say that to all the guys," Dad said.

"Only the cute ones," Pat winked.

The humor brightened my spirits. If he could carry on like that, maybe he wasn't as sick as he looked.

"I'm a little tired," Dad said after ten minutes or so. "Nancy, I love you. Want you to know."

Tears filled my eyes. He had never said those words to me. Though I had complained to Mom many times about his reserve, she always answered, "It's just not his way. But you know he loves you."

As much as I wanted to hear the words, when it happened, it disappointed me. His voice sounded weird, drugged. Mom put an arm around my shoulder for comfort.

I stayed home for a week. I was either at the hospital or planning meals at home while Mom taught. Richie and Sally went to their high school classes. Plus, Mom had an evening class once a week—her last course prior to graduation. She worried about how she could do it all and considered dropping out. Dad insisted she stick with it. "Enough torture," he said.

One night after visiting Dad, Mom hurried through the waiting room. "Elise (Eeelise)," a male voice called out.

She turned to find Harlan, the FHA board member who headed our farm inspection, standing over a magazine rack. "Oh, Harlan. What are you doing here?"

"My wife has . . . cancer. She's been here for several weeks." His head dropped. "I'm so sorry to hear about Rich. He's so young to have all this happen."

She thought he might cry. She realized that his soft-spoken nature and few words had kept her from ever really having a conversation with him. Instead, she had assessed him purely on his physical characteristics: short, mostly bald, and stocky. It struck her that he was a genuine and caring man.

Mom nodded. "It's as hard for the family as it is for the patient. I'm sure you feel that way too."

Harlan assured Mom he would handle everything with FHA on the farm loan, if there were questions or concerns. She thanked him for his help.

They visited a while longer, then Harlan held out his hand out as they parted. "Be sure and give Rich my best. I have always admired him."

Richie stayed quiet that week—even to me. I helped him with chores, and sat on a stool in the milking parlor while he cleaned up the hoses and milking machines. I wanted assurance that he wasn't scared in order to lessen my own fear. But he didn't offer any encouragement—instead he frowned more and laughed less.

I walked out to the barn with him the night before I left to go back to Hillsdale. We always did a final check of the barn and calf pens before heading back to the house. The crisp air and slight breeze helped keep the manure smell in check.

"School will be out in eight weeks. I can help you this summer," I said.

"You think you're any better at driving the tractor?" he said. The change in his somber expression delighted me. I jabbed him.

For eight long weeks, Richie ran the farm with the help of Earl, a local high school boy. Mom says Richie never complained about a thing. Earl was as capable as Richie around animals and machinery, and he possessed the same strong work ethic. From time to time he teased Richie the way boys do. Earl got him laughing again.

When Dad returned home from the hospital, he weighed 152 pounds. He was hardly recognizable, with his gaunt face, sagging muscles and shortness of breath. Life changed—for all of us.

Shortly after Dad's return he and Mom visited a heart specialist in Cleveland to learn more about his prognosis At the time, we were told they had a doctor's appointment there, nothing more.

Recently Mom told me about the appointment that day. Both sat nervously in the waiting room crowded with elderly patients slumped in their chairs. It wasn't an atmosphere of hope. Once inside the doctor's office, it only worsened.

The doctor picked up Dad's X-rays. He moved from one to another and then back again, examining them for what felt like an eternity. Finally, he turned the light off and returned the X-ray to its envelope.

"Richard, I won't sugar coat this," he began. "With the amount of damage you had, it's a miracle you're alive."

Mom said for some reason his remark made her feel optimistic.

"Basically, your heart looks like a sponge. You're young, fit and there's no evidence to determine why this happened. Bad genes? Who knows. All I can say is that there is so much scar tissue damage that what you need is a whole new heart, as if that were an option," the doctor said sarcastically.

Dad didn't flinch. Mom cried.

"How much time, doc?" Dad asked.

The doctor cleared his throat. "Two days? Two months? Who knows. Definitely not more than two years. Get your affairs in order. Enjoy your hobbies."

Dad grinned. "That would be riding my motorcycle and flying my airplane."

"Oh God no, neither of those," the doctor said.

Mom said the ride back to the farm never took longer. Neither said much. Mom drove while Dad dozed or gazed at the countryside. Summer was a promise away.

"It's pretty this time of the year, don't you think? Maybe we could go up to Lake Erie for a picnic some time," Mom said.

"Lots of good memories there," he said casually before pointing out a new barn. "See that over there? That's state of the art."

Mom kept her eyes on the road. "Shall we keep this just between us?"

"Definitely. I want everyone to treat me normally," Dad said.

Dad stood next to the hangar and watched the forty-year-old buyer, only a few years younger than him, fly the Cessna 180 away. Mom hung back at the car. He put his head down then and cried for the first time since the heart attack. When he dropped to his knees, Mom ran to his side.

"I'm sorry, El. So sorry. I wanted to give you so much. I ran out of time," he cried against her chest.

"You've given me everything. I love you. We have great kids. And who knows, the doctor could be wrong. Miracles happen every day," she said and wiped away his tears.

Lilly visited more than usual. She tried to adhere to healthy treats but her taste ran more to prime rib, éclairs, and homemade ice cream. In the past Dad's eyes always lit up when she appeared with some new delight. But his attitude changed and she noticed it right away. He hardly said a word to anyone. He slept a lot, which was also unusual.

Mom said that Lilly cried whenever just the two of them were together. "What can we do, Elise? His humor is gone, he doesn't seem interested in anything. Not even the Percherons."

Lilly pressed her about what the heart specialist had said. Mom squirmed out of telling the complete truth.

"The doctor didn't have the best bedside manner. He thought Rich should change his lifestyle and eat healthy," Mom said.

"And that would make him well?" Lilly asked like someone grasping for the smallest ray of hope.

"We have to be supportive. Not act sad. He's blue because he had to sell the airplane. We all have to adjust," Mom said.

Before the end of my first year of college Mom was invited to join an honorary teacher's sorority, Delta Kappa Gamma. The assistant superintendent, Mrs. Lizotte, was the president at the time and had observed Mom teaching for ten years. She nominated Mom for the honor, citing her exemplary diligence and leadership outside the classroom.

Mom felt proud, but believed the timing was bad. She told Mrs. Lizotte that she didn't know how she could possibly accept another commitment with Dad's uncertain health issues.

"Elise, that's precisely why you need this now," Mrs. Lizotte said.

After being home for the summer for a couple of weeks, my grades arrived in the mail. I had already spoken to an admissions officer at Miami University without telling Mom or Dad. It appeared that I would be able to transfer there if my grades were over a 3.0. My stomach flip-flopped the day I opened the mailbox and saw the envelope with Hillsdale's emblem. I ripped it open—3.5—I'd made the dean's list! I glowed and pranced into the house.

Dad didn't say a word. No congratulations, no smiles, nothing. It crushed me. Unbeknownst to me, he grappled with his own mortality while I focused only on my problems, my issues.

"Now I can go to a better school. Cheaper, even," I informed my parents at dinner that night. Dad looked right through me.

"Where?" he asked. I told him and he nodded. "That's fine. If that's what you want." His quick acceptance was somewhat surprising.

Why wouldn't Dad acknowledge my hard work? I had never been such a disciplined student before, and he knew it. I cornered Mom. She assured me that he just wasn't himself. At first I didn't buy it. We argued, and I accused her of defending him.

"Nancy, I went to college for ten years to finish my degree. I didn't go to the graduation because your dad was in the hospital. He never, ever said one word of praise to me. Not to this day."

Her eyes filled with tears. It floored me. My accomplishment was a sprint compared to her marathon. I hugged her. "You're right, Mom, he's not himself."

The FHA board met the first of every month to determine which farms to inspect. Every veteran who obtained one of its low-interest loans got used to the government checking in regularly. If a farmer struggled, the board used resources at its disposal to help him. But a nonworking farm made the note due and payable.

One day Richie backed up the tractor to hitch up a wagon. I held the tongue and waited to drop in the pin when the holes aligned. Both of us looked up when a station wagon pulled into the driveway.

"The FHA board," Richie mumbled as I squinted. "Must be inspection time." Richie turned off the ignition on the Oliver Super 88.

Harlan climbed out of the car, ahead of the other members, to face Nippy, our aptly named dog. Most everyone respected her bark, especially when she bared her teeth. But Harlan never shied away. He stood and let her circle; she continued barking while he talked softly to her. After several minutes, she lost interest and raced off to chase one of the barn cats.

"Richie," Harlan called out. "Just wanted to see how your dad's doing."

"Not too good, I'm afraid," Richie answered. "His spirits have been low since he had to sell the plane."

Harlan raised his eyebrows. "I'm sorry. Wish I would have gone for that ride he promised."

The pair stood in awkward silence. I thought Harlan wanted to say more. He looked out toward the barnyard.

Richie told Harlan to go ahead and look around. I hopped up on the wagon and watched Harlan and the other board members walk toward the barn.

"He's a nice man. Do you know how his wife is doing?" I asked.

Richie told me she had died in the hospital while Dad was there. "He still has two young sons to raise," he added.

Dad had kept Mom's gift of the used motorcycle for a year after she gave it to him as a Christmas gift before trading it in for the biggest, blackest Harley Davidson he could find. It was a monster of a bike for Dad and a real stretch for Richie with his skinny, five-foot-nine frame. But Dad pushed Richie to learn to ride it anyhow.

A week after Dad came home from the hospital, Richie rode on a dirt road not far from the farm. He hit some loose gravel going too fast on a hairpin turn. Using the hand brake, he skidded into a ditch. He smashed through the windshield and slid across the rocky shoulder of the road, finally coming to a stop on top of the bike. There was blood everywhere, but he said his first concern was the motorcycle. He propped the bike up, started it miraculously, and rode the mile home at half speed.

As Richie drove in, I was weeding in the garden. I could tell the bike was banged up. I ran to shed where he stored the bike. The windshield was gone, Richie's T-shirt was torn to shreds, and dried blood covered his arm and back.

"Holy crap! What happened?" I yelled.

"Crashed. Nance, I need your help. Get towels, soap and water and alcohol. I'll wait for you here," he winced.

I scurried to the house and rounded up the supplies. Dad called from the bedroom and asked if that was Richie he'd heard drive in. I made up something and ran back to the shed, where Richie paced. He removed what was left of the tee shirt and stood over the workbench. He gripped its edge like he was preparing for a whipping.

With a wet towel and butterfly touches, I dabbed at the wounds. He cried when I got to the alcohol. We were so engrossed in his treatment that we didn't hear the footsteps.

"What's going on in here?" Mom said before she noticed the damage.

Richie waved at me to continue. "It looks bad, Ma. I'll be okay. Just a little accident with the Harley."

Mom wiped her forehead as if to say, "What else?" She silently watched us handle the crisis, then she inspected the bike.

"If I get a new windshield and touch up the fender, I don't think Dad will be too angry. I'm so mad at myself. Dad sure doesn't need this right now," Richie said.

"Your dad will be glad you weren't hurt," Mom said.

Richie waited a day. It took him two attempts to get the confession out. After he spilled the whole story, Dad kind of smiled.

"Now I have an excuse to trade it in on an Electroglide. Since I'm not strong enough to crank-start it with my leg. Besides, an accident here and there is part of learning to ride," Dad said.

Richie shoved his hands in his pockets. "Do you think Dr. Glosh is okay with you riding the bike?"

"A man has to have something to look forward to," Dad replied. "Besides, the motorcycle isn't any more dangerous than driving a car."

Mom kept us all going through that long, solemn summer. But there were no jokes, no teasing, and no fun. I wanted our old life back—we all did. I transferred to Miami University and secretly welcomed the chance to escape the tense home situation for a while.

Dad had accepted my change of colleges in stride, but as I got settled in, he rarely asked me a thing about my courses or what the new school was like.

During that academic year, Earl continued to help Richie, and eventually Dad resumed milking the cows. It cheered him up to be able to work again, even though the boys handled the heaviest physical chores.

Richie and Dad worked with the Percherons in order to show them at the Ohio State Fair the next summer. The more progress they made with each of the horses, the happier Dad became.

When Richie started his senior year in high school, he told Dad his intention to study engineering at college. It helped Dad's morale. Dad encouraged him to look at Purdue, Michigan State, and the University of Michigan. For some reason, he didn't suggest his alma mater, Case Institute, because he believed there were too many "brainy kids." He wanted Richie to have a well-rounded environment. Dad asked me to take the road trip with Richie to visit the three potential schools.

Michigan State had the prettiest campus, Michigan had the prestigious name, and Purdue had concrete.

Richie laughed at my summary as we drove back to the farm. "Good to know how you pick a college," he joked. But then he got serious. "I think Dad and I will decide, but I wish I didn't have to go. I'd really like to stay on the farm."

In the end, Richie and Dad chose Purdue. I liked the idea because my sorority had a chapter there and I'd have a place to stay when I visited.

I tried to pump him up with all the fun he'd have. All the Big Ten football games and no chores.

"You're not like me," he countered. "Or, I'm not like you."

That spring Dad shared a secret with Richie. "I've *arranged* for Nancy to be Percheron Queen at the Ohio State Fair." Richie laughed and questioned Dad about the wisdom of that decision. But Dad assured him that he knew me well. "She'd love to be queen of anything, bud. Trust me on this. But don't say anything. I want to surprise her with it when she comes home for summer break."

Richie kept the secret. So did Mom. Nobody breathed a word—so Dad got his wish of announcing the surprise to me.

Every once in a while, the memory of my "reign" still makes me laugh. Dad knew me. The thought of wearing a crown appealed to me so much that I fantasized about it all that summer. I pictured a packed arena, and some kind of elevated stand where I would sit and smile, departing only long enough to hand out trophies to the winners. Flashbulbs would go off. Someone might ask for my autograph.

The gap between my active imagination and the reality of that day was enormous. In truth, my big day was more of an embarrassment than anything else. There was no parade float or other notoriety to illuminate my title. Dad had said I would be presenting awards. I almost bolted when I saw the nearly empty arena with no elevated stand to separate me from the crowd. The only thing in abundance was the powerful stench of sweaty animals. The first time I presented a ribbon to a winner my high heels sunk and nearly stuck in the dirt of the show ring, causing snickers from the gallery. Looking back on it, I prefer to say that once upon a time, in my youth, I was queen for a day.

Likewise, Dad's horses didn't fare as well as he hoped. He hadn't planned on the fierce competition from the other owners who had bred and shown horses for years. They had a flair for the event—they braided the horses' manes, oiled their coats until they glistened, and most of the men wore fancy sport coats or elaborate shirts. Dad dressed in clean and pressed khakis. He said the judges didn't care about all of that "hogwash" but given the outcome, I'd say he greatly underestimated it.

Two days after the fair, I returned to Miami University for my junior year. Readying himself for his own entry into college life at Purdue, Richie packed for several days but didn't talk to anyone. Mom says to this day that she felt like she was sending him to prison. Even the fact that Richie would be rooming with Jim, a high school friend, didn't cheer him up.

Mom and Sally planned to drive Richie to Lafayette, Indiana, and return back to Ohio all in one day, which was too strenuous of a journey for Dad.

That morning, Richie broke down and cried at breakfast. Sally ate her shredded wheat without looking up and Mom didn't know what to say.

Dad finished packing the car and stood close by. He waited for Richie. They shook hands and then Dad hugged him. "You watch out for all those college girls," he said with a smile, choking back tears.

Richie dropped his head and climbed into the car.

Homesickness plagued Richie from the outset. We all tried to comfort him. Mom and Dad called him every week, Lilly made chocolate chip cookies, and I wrote. But the sadness persisted.

"How about I come up there for homecoming?" I offered.

The idea of a major football game in a real stadium with thousands of fans appealed to me. More than that, Richie said there were ten guys to every girl at Purdue. I liked that too.

It was a sunny crisp day when I arrived in Lafayette. Excitement and enthusiastic alumni lingered on every corner. I led him around as if I attended there, too. He didn't seem to know much about his school because he had not made any effort to explore the campus outside of the halls where his classes were.

"Let's check out the student union," I said.

We found a bowling alley and fell into childhood competition. He smiled and seemed to enjoy it.

"How are the classes going?" I asked as we sipped Cokes after our game.

"I'm pretty much struggling with everything," he said. "Especially physics, not to mention strength of materials. Y' know, just the courses that are building blocks for engineering. Maybe I should drive a truck," he smirked.

When I suggested a talk with his advisor Richie shook his head. Dr. Perdoff was both a pompous jerk *and* the professor of the class he was failing.

"Every time I meet with the guy he acts disgusted and reminds me how all of his other advisees are on the Dean's List," he said.

"Maybe you just need time to adjust. Don't give up, you were always a good student," I said.

Springtime brought hope. Earl practically ran the entire farm; after two years, Dad had finally accepted his debilitated life, and Mom taught school. With Sally in high school and Richie and I in college, things quieted around the house. Mom said it was eerie. But everyone adapted to the changes.

I felt so optimistic that I made plans to work at a Michigan resort the next summer. Dad thought he'd be able to operate the farm's machinery by then.

The phone rang late one night, halfway through my finals. I bolted from my top bunk and hurried to answer. No one called at that hour with good news. I jerked the receiver off the hook.

"Nancy," Mom's voice said and then she sobbed.

I held the phone tight against my ear and slid down the wall. "Please don't say it, Mom," I said.

My three roommates had woken up and surrounded me. Their faces paled as they interpreted the severity of the call.

Mom blew her nose. "Your dad passed away. A few hours ago."

I remember I asked questions as if the answers would make a difference in the outcome. Where? How? What will happen to us?

Mom told me that Sally had found him in the barn with his horses. He hadn't come in for dinner, so she'd gone looking for him. He didn't answer when she called out. She found him near the water tank. Maybe he had tried to revive himself.

I sobbed. My roommates cried. I wondered if they worried because it could happen to them.

"Mom, does Richie know?"

Mom said he was already on a bus headed for home and that he'd be there in the morning. I worried about him and wished I could be with him.

I gasped for air and tried to calm myself. "Mom, did you know he was this bad?"

She hesitated. "We knew there had been irreversible damage. That he didn't have much time. He wanted to live out his life being active. You know how he was."

That last word—was—hit me hard.

Family, friends, farm neighbors, and Dad's navy cohorts, and Case classmates packed Lodi Methodist Church. Mom tended to us kids and kept her own feelings in check. The sad day started early and lingered, like bad news. Nothing comforted us, especially Richie. His sobs reverberated throughout the sanctuary. Our tear-stained cheeks and slumped shoulders discouraged well-meaning mourners from offering very lengthy expressions of sympathy.

Uncle Chase and Aunt Kitty comforted Mom with their presence. The two of them took over the household and managed phone calls. I remember that they wanted Mom to rest but she refused. Each one vowed to return to help her with whatever needed to be done.

Mom's said that she cherished the outpouring of support but deep inside, she knew she'd have to do it herself. By herself.

*   *   *

Dr. Glosh phoned Mom a week after the service. "I want you to come in. We need to talk," he said.

Mom's said his request perplexed her, but she complied. She trusted his expertise and respected his kind bedside manner. He had cried at the funeral just like many others.

Being in the waiting room brought back strange feelings for Mom. She was not accustomed to being the patient. She had gotten used to accompanying Dad on his many visits over the previous two years.

"Elise," Dr. Glosh began, once they were seated in his office. "Have you cried?"

Mom shook her head. "Not a drop. I feel numb."

The doctor glanced up at a flickering light. "Tell you what. I'm going to step out of the room and I want you to cry. You have my permission. And make it a good one. I'll be back in a while."

Mom says the door hadn't closed all the way when she crumbled to the floor. She cried so hard her hair hurt. It scared her. She thought she might never stop, so deep was her grief.

After a time, Dr. Glosh tapped lightly on the door and entered. "Much better. You can't keep those feelings trapped inside, it's not healthy." He patted her shoulder.

Two weeks after the funeral, and after all of her support network had returned to their own lives, we struggled to put our family back together. One night Richie wandered into the master bedroom where Mom sat propped up in the old walnut bed rereading sympathy cards.

"Richie, would you like to see these?" she asked.

He shook his head. "Mom, I don't want you to ever call me that again. Ever." He started to leave the room.

His strong tone shocked her. The mild-mannered, obedient child had raised his voice to her only once before. She moved to the middle of the bed and made room for him. She patted the space and pleaded. "Please, sit down."

"I didn't ask for this, Mom. Dad's gone. Now I have to take over. I'm *Rich* from now on. Tell everyone, okay?"

She blinked back tears. "Of course. I understand."

They maintained eye contact until his eyes drifted toward the dresser, Dad's dresser. A pocket knife, a book of matches, and some change sat on top, just as he had left it. Rich rose and fingered the items. He stood there a while.

"What are we going to do?" he asked as he inspected the dresser like it was a precious relic.

Mom gathered up the cards and set them aside. "I need to sell the farm, pretty soon."

Rich shook his head. "No. I can run it. We could keep it, Mom. I hate college, more than I can tell you."

"Farming is hard work. Your dad wanted more for you. For all of you." She hesitated and watched him for a bit.

He stood silent.

"Rich, I'll tell you what. I'll let you decide and we'll do whatever you think is best. Okay?" Mom said.

Part IV

Atlanta, 1942-45

Before Rich left for training at Pensacola he asked if Elise would write to him. She agreed—much in the same way, or so she thought, that she exchanged letters with another navy man, named Dan, whom she'd dated just once after Peter left for the army. It was common during World War II for young women to have pen pals in the military—most of Elise's girlfriends corresponded with men too. They felt sorry for the servicemen, who were homesick and off defending the country without female companionship. The occasional letter gave the men something to look forward to.

Dan's letters came once a week, while a letter from Rich arrived daily. She thought it was a bit much, but he had a lot to say and she knew it boosted his spirit to have someone to write to. Still, no matter how often Rich wrote, she usually sat down just once a week and answered both of the navy men. She never considered that the exchanges were anything more than friendly and, perhaps, her duty as a citizen. Once she even mixed up her responses to Rich's and Dan's letters. Both men took it in stride, but later Dad kidded her for years with, "Who's Dan? I must have made quite an impression if you forgot my name so quickly."

Meanwhile, Peter's letters that arrived every other day filled her emotional and romantic needs. They were short of military detail and long on adoration. In his lovesick outpourings, Peter obsessed over the plans for their married life and how happy they'd be once they were by each other's side. He recalled dances they'd been to, fun times with Eugenia and Jimmie, and told her how much he couldn't wait to hold her again.

All of the letters became an escape for Elise, something to look forward to each day after chauffeuring Pops to his daily radiation treatments at

Emory and then on to Georgia Savings Bank. She worried about his pain or tiredness after each procedure, but he assured her he'd be fine.

"The whole thing is free," he boasted to Elise during one of their car rides. "They're making me a test case since they say they've never seen this kind of cancer in someone's mouth."

She wanted him to say they could cure him, but he always stopped short of such a promise. In fact, he said the doctors didn't give him much of a chance at all.

"Maybe they just don't want you to be overly optimistic," Elise said.

Pops chuckled. "No, I think they truly believe I'm hopeless. No matter. I will be their first success and then they'll write about me in the textbooks. Sure hope they include some of my better jokes."

The time spent driving, waiting at the lab, and then dropping Pops at the bank took three hours out of Elise's day. She'd hurry home, hoping for a letter from one of her suitors. Without her friends and the routine of college life, she often felt at a loss for what to do with herself.

So when Elise saw that Southern Bell was advertising an opening for a part-time job in their mapping department, she applied. Atlanta teemed with new construction and growth, yet there were not enough men available for work—and most businesses were desperate for help. At first, the job sounded too technical to Elise, although she liked the man who interviewed her, as well as two female employees she met who were her age. The hours fit perfectly with the commitment she'd made to Pops, and she desperately craved something to occupy her mind. She accepted the job.

To Elise's surprise, the job turned out to offer more than a way to kill time. She developed a newfound confidence and pride in earning her own money and being part of a team.

The manager must have realized rather quickly that Elise's easy-going disposition and sense of responsibility were major assets, since she received a raise in her second month of employment.

After five months of treatments, Pops' cheek began to cave in. The therapy, given outside the mouth through a kind of x-ray, took its toll. Even though the procedure was painless, his skin had slowly sloughed away, leaving a hole in his cheek. Soon Pops' diet was limited to pureed food, like you'd prepare for a baby, or soup. A patch covered the hole while he struggled with his meals, without complaint. The doctors had anticipated such a by-product of the strong radiation treatments, just not so soon. Still, everyone agreed to continue with the program.

"I'm going to beat this disease," Pops said.

The hole grew from the size of a penny to that of a fifty-cent piece, and Pops began to talk lopsided. He never felt embarrassed by the disfigurement, however—just frustrated that it was so hard to talk. And talking was one of his favorite pastimes.

*　　*　　*

In 1968, a year after his death, Mom gave me a cardboard box filled with Dad's letters during one of my visits to Ohio. The box sat at the foot of the bed in the guest room. She noticed my quizzical look while she helped me unpack.

"Those are your dad's letters," she said. "It's not so good for me to have them around right now."

I thought she should keep them in storage nearby, when rereading them later on might offer some peace or, perhaps, closure. But she insisted I take the box, as long as I promised not to destroy it.

"You'll learn a lot about your father," she said.

Love letters—that's what I assumed they were. But they were like a journal of all that was happening in the world, the war, and the progression of their relationship. The letters started in 1942 and continued through their courtship, marriage, and my birth. For thirty years, I would pull one out here and there. But nothing compelled me to stick with it and read all of them. Not until 2005 when I reopened the box and put them in chronological order. Somehow I was ready. It took me a week to read all of them, and each day I was surprised by something I learned about my father as a mature young man. As his daughter, I had witnessed his strength and compassion, but I had no idea about the depth of his sentimental and emotional side. He was utterly devoted to family and had little patience for those who wasted time and energy on frivolous activities.

"I can't believe how these fellows act so irresponsibly," he'd written of his fellow servicemen. "They cash their paychecks and hurry off to drink and spend it on women who are only interested in a good time. Most of them are married and don't seem to take their situation seriously. Given where we are and our mission, I would think they'd consider how fragile life is and be more mature. I certainly don't intend to leave such a sorry legacy if something unfortunate should happen to me."

Given his pragmatic view of the brevity of life, it made me wonder if he knew somehow his life would be cut short.

*   *   *

As spring progressed into the thick heat of summer 1942, Rich continued to write Elise daily. He explained to her that the navy pilot program lived by the rule of "survival of the strongest by weeding out the weak." If he avoided being eliminated, then he'd begin an intensive seven-month course nicknamed the "Annapolis of the Air." Only upon completion of that grueling step would he received his wings as a naval aviator and be promoted to ensign. His ambition didn't stop there however—he wanted to fly fighter planes.

"The navy considers me too old at twenty-six, they want young guys," he wrote. "But I'll make them change their minds. They definitely test what you're made of and I am positive they will come to know yours truly."

What he didn't mention in his letters was that the navy also wanted men who were single. The statistic of a pilot dying every thirteen minutes was accurate.

The journalistic reports of his training made the distant war a reality, and this frightened Elise. In one letter he described the operation of a machine gun in such detail that he seemed detached from its potential for harm.

Every letter told a story of how the navy challenged them, probing for physical or mental weakness. Rich didn't fret over it but felt sorry for the constant stream of guys "busted out." He exercised, tried to get proper sleep, and closely adhered to the surgeon general's advice of no alcohol, cigarettes, or overeating, which he followed pretty much his entire life.

"You sure don't want to end up in sick bay because the doctors take any small excuse to inspect you head to toe," he wrote. "One fellow busted out after being detained in the hospital for a week. He got so far behind, he never caught up."

He shared volumes about the beauty and freedom of flying, saying that he knew there was more to life when he was up there.

Elise wasn't sure if he meant God or something spiritual. They'd not yet discussed religion. Several letters later, he wrote about the irony of having a chapel on the base, right in the midst of where men learned the art of defensive and offensive warring methods. He felt conflicted.

"A person volunteering his services without faith in some supreme being is doing so in vain, but maybe the fellows don't like the services," he wrote. "I can believe without being in the church."

The only personal remarks always came at the end of the letter. He mentioned how he was comforted by having her lovely picture on his bureau and knowing he had a little redhead pulling for him. All the letters in those first four months ended with "lots of luck and good health . . . Sincerely, Rich."

Nana knew about the letters from both navy men, as well as those from Peter. Once in a while she asked Elise how Rich's training was progressing or if his family worried about him potentially going into harm's way.

Nana either left Peter's mail on Elise's bureau or simply handed it over to her, but if it was a letter from Rich, she'd beam. "Another letter from Rich, Elise!" As much as Elise still loved Peter, Nana was relentless in her objection.

"When are you going to break up with him for good? I'm telling you he is not the right man for you," Nana said so frequently that Elise was often upset and uneasy. Elise wanted to tell Nana that she still had Peter's engagement ring, but she was afraid of her mother's reaction, although she said she never lied about the lingering relationship.

*   *   *

Rich had been in Pensacola four months when he invited Elise to visit him for a weekend, something Peter had never done. When Elise broached the topic with her mother, Nana refused to even consider it. In those days, young single women usually deferred to their parents when making such plans.

She avoided eye contact with Elise as she stood up and fussed with her customary dark rayon dress. She shrugged her right shoulder and cleared her throat a few times. With a completely blank expression and her mouth drawn in a thin tight line, Nana finally responded: "Elise, all men have only one thing on their mind. It's not appropriate for a young lady to visit a man unaccompanied and stay in a hotel. He can wait until his next leave to see you—please convey that he's welcome to stay with us here in Atlanta then."

Elise wanted to go to Pensacola and was disappointed with Nana's decision. The idea of the ocean, warmer weather, and getting out of Atlanta for a little break sounded great. She knew Rich was a gentleman and that Nana worried needlessly.

Rich, however, took the news in stride and began to plan. In fact, he agreed somewhat with Nana's assessment of men. "I don't blame your mother for being uncomfortable about the situation," he wrote. "The fellows do a lot of strange things down here, usually involving alcohol and women. And since she doesn't know me very well, I can't call her unreasonable."

One month later, Rich wrote that he had a week's leave upcoming and planned to spend the entire time in Atlanta. Elise eagerly anticipated the visit, but at the same time felt guilty over the developing romantic dilemma. Although she and Rich had only seen each other a few times before he departed for flight school, she felt like she knew him well after four months of exchanging letters. Rich expressed himself better in writing than verbally—his letters were thoughtful, carefully shaped, and revealed his truest feelings and beliefs. Elise liked what she had come to know about this quiet, genuine man. Still, she was also a little nervous—a week could feel like a month if things didn't go well.

The day Elise picked up Rich at the train station, her fears dissipated. He was more handsome than she recalled, and she ran to hug him. He held her for a bit and gave her a passionate kiss. Elise was momentarily surprised by her forwardness, but was too giddy about Rich's affection to worry much about it.

The pair spent most of the week talking. Rich questioned Elise about her views on the war, marriage, and children. He listened intently, without a single interruption. She'd never known a man so curious about how women thought about things. He said he considered women to be man's better half, and he understood that a woman could only make a guy better.

"I've never known a woman like you," he told her. "And listening to the lilt in your voice is the icing on the cake."

She began to feel differently about him. She was physically attracted to him and he seemed so mature. He knew exactly what he wanted for his future—a wife and children. The conversations with Rich made her realize how much she and Peter had never discussed. She wondered what Peter thought about having children, but she had never asked him.

Rich asked her things about womanhood and what made it hard. She began to think more seriously about life because of what he wanted to know.

Elise had thought of life in a more carefree way until that time. She loved to be with her friends and have fun, thinking of herself more as girl than woman. Rich talked about life with a partner, a friend, a lover, and a confidant. As much as he delved into the deep issues of life, he could instantly see the humor as well.

He laughed when Elise told him about the Sunday rides to the country that her family had taken when she was a child, and how the whole time she'd wondered how long it would be before they got back to the city for ice cream. "They do have ice cream in the country now," he teased her.

Rich and Elise both shared tight bonds with their families. Rich greatly respected his mother and two sisters. He talked about them with such insight and humor that she wanted to meet them. One day, when she asked him to name each woman's strongest trait, he paused for a while. After pondering for a bit, he answered that Lilly (his mother) had a big heart, Sis had brains and ambition—not to mention an infectious laugh—while Peg, the youngest, was the beauty.

"What's your father like?" Elise asked.

Rich stared at the floor. The silence lasted long enough to be uncomfortable. Finally he said, "My dad is hard. And hard of hearing."

Elise thought he was just teasing again, exaggerating to be funny.

Rich looked up and held her gaze. "My dad and I don't see eye-to-eye on much. He's never been happy with any of my decisions. Plus, I sure got my share of lickings growing up." He forced a smile. "Bet you never had even one."

Mom told him about the one and only time. "Mother and Pops never had to say much to me to get me to mind. I was so sensitive and shy. My daddy always fancied himself quite the disciplinarian, but he had more smoke than fire. Mother has really always been the stern one. Even now I'm a little afraid of her."

Rich shook his head. "It's the opposite for me . . . Mom's easy. And I don't think she ever considered spanking any of us."

A breeze flowed through the back screen door and caused it to bang. They decided it was a signal to move outside and enjoy a lovely day. Dad suggested a game of gin rummy, boasting that he was a champion card player.

Rich and Elise were so comfortable with each other that the week flew by in no time. But even with the ease and enjoyment of the visit, she wasn't sure how strongly she felt about him. She knew she was drawn to him and had even hoped he might sneak into her room late at night for some kissing. She found herself mildly disappointed when he remained such a proper gentleman throughout the visit. And deep down she craved her mother's approval of the man she married; Nana was clearly impressed by Rich, so Elise had continued getting to know him. Yet she held fast to a glimmer of hope that Nana might change her mind about Peter.

Rich reminisced about the Atlanta trip in his letters for weeks afterward. He surprised Elise with his interest in her hometown and culture: "This week I read *Gone with the Wind* in my spare time. I only wish I'd read that fine book when I was in Atlanta so I could have asked you my numerous questions about the various skirmishes, homes, etc. It's rather hard to visualize the fighting was so close to the center of town when considering Atlanta's size today. I'm glad I took the time to read it as it helps to explain so many of the Southern customs and traditions of which previously (sorry to say) I was quite ignorant."

Elise continued to juggle work, chauffeuring for Pops, and reading and answering letters. Once in a while she met up with her friend Emma, who had met Rich at their first Sunday dinner, and she remembered how handsome he was.

"Do you think Rich is in love with you?" Emma quizzed Elise one day as they sipped Cokes at Medlock's drug store. "I mean, heck, you might be forced to choose."

Elise fidgeted with her sweater. "He's more serious than I am, but the more I get to know Rich the more attractive he is to me. And then there's all the problem with my mother."

Emma puzzled. "You mean because she doesn't like Peter?"

Elise nodded. "And you're right. Sooner or later I will have to choose. I wish I could put them together and make one fellow."

"All I know is that I've never had two men fighting over me," Emma lamented.

The radiation treatments that Pops endured for a year proved successful: eventually, the cancer was gone. Pops assured the doctor it wasn't just medicine that had healed him but his deep faith. The atheist doctor scoffed at the statement but later attended the family's church for the first time.

Though he was cured, the unsightly hole remained in Pops' cheek. Sometimes he wore a gauze bandage over it and sometimes he just left it natural. A plastic surgeon assured him that it could be fixed by grafting skin from Pops' chest.

Elise was relieved to hear there was a cosmetic and functional solution. She was ashamed of how uncomfortable she was being in public with Pops and observing how people stared at him. Surprisingly, Nana—who was so fastidious and critical of her own appearance and that of others—showed no reaction to Pops' disfigurement. She looked right past it as if nothing had changed, and she never said a word about it. This made Elise all the more guilty about her own discomfort with his appearance.

The operation was lengthy, and Elise nearly fainted when she saw Pops in the recovery area. The graft was a rope-like piece of skin that the surgeon had coiled until the hole disappeared. The reddened substitute hung loose, ugly, and rough. Pops didn't seem fazed. Instead, he was excited that he'd soon be eating Claudie's fried chicken again.

The wound never fully healed, nor did the color, texture, or looseness of the skin improve. People reacted with more horror to the graft than they had to the hole, which Pops did notice. He took to wearing a bandage, holding his head with his good side toward the listener, or sometimes holding a handkerchief over the scar to ease the onlooker's discomfort.

Elise described Pops' condition in letters to Rich, who sympathized with her dismay. He wrote, "Medicine is a wonderful thing. I'm sure some day there will be a way to better his appearance. And Elise, I'm sure your father wants you to be optimistic."

*　　*　　*

Four months after Elise met Rich, Peter wrote her that the signal corps had finally moved him from behind a desk at Fort Jackson to radio repair school at Ft. Monmouth, New Jersey. Following that six-month course, he would go directly into officer candidate school (OCS), meaning he would not be able to see Elise until October 1942. He joked that at least she would be marrying an officer.

Today, when Peter talks about Elise's letters, I understand how they were lifelines for him. He would reread each letter several times and then add to a bundled stack. Often, if time permitted, he'd reread all the letters he had accumulated thus far.

"She always wrote the most encouraging things about what I was studying and said she admired my mind for technical things," he said. "I studied hard since I was the youngest guy in the unit. I knew it would help me land a good job after the war."

As Peter relayed the events from his perspective that had taken place more than fifty years earlier, his haunted tone saddened me. "You had no idea about another man, nothing at all?" I asked. His head dropped before he answered a faint no.

Since their first kiss and Elise's disclosure about being engaged to Peter, Rich had never brought it up again. She surmised he truly believed his prediction of, "We'll just see about that."

What started out as being hospitality to a serviceman had morphed into something serious. Elise felt sneaky—each letter from Rich or Peter intensified the confusion and pressure.

Rich's letters continued to talk about all he was learning in ground school, his adventures when off duty, and his interest in the environment, agriculture, and wildlife.

By the end of the summer, however, his letters began to gather emotional steam. He elaborated on how well he had come to know Elise through their letters: "If this is the only way to learn about the one you love, then so be it. And you, Elise, are everything I thought I wanted to meet. Until you, every woman seemed false. Somehow you have deciphered the secret to these old heart strings."

He went on to recall the first time he had kissed her and how he just couldn't help himself. He told her not to worry about his pushing for something more because he had the utmost respect for her. His sign-off changed to *Love, Rich*.

When Elise read those last two words—"Love Rich"—she realized the extent of her dilemma. She felt deep respect and attraction for Rich. She was falling in love with him. And yet she was devastated about the possibility of breaking things off with Peter. When she thought about how homesick and heartfelt he was, the guilt almost crushed her. The outpourings of love in Peter's letters had begun to make her sad, though, because she realized she didn't feel the same way about him any more. Her love for him felt adolescent in some way.

In his very next letter, Rich admitted how he was often at a loss for words when face to face with a person. He apologized for his shortcoming, but assured Elise that she made him feel safe and comfortable, and he wanted to learn to be more expressive.

"All I can say is that I love you. Please keep the faith and let's see how things develop," he wrote.

Elise eventually began signing her letters to him *Love, Elise*, but she worried about the weight of the word "love."

In early September, Rich returned to Atlanta for another week-long visit. Again, Elise thrilled at the sight of him. For the first time she saw him his dress whites—with his blond hair and tanned skin, he was quite dashing. Not that he ever noticed the stares he got from other women. Sometimes Elise pointed out a good-looking woman who was checking him out. He always dismissed it and said he was with the only girl he wanted. She liked that.

Nana and Pops outdid themselves on Rich's second visit. There was extra shopping for special menus: roast beef, ingredients for Charlotte Russes (fancy dessert cakes), and fresh vegetables. When Rich arrived they announced their plans for a day trip and picnic to Roswell, Georgia, where he could learn something of the Hunter heritage. Roswell King, Elise's great, great-grandfather, had founded the town. They also wanted to take him to their church, Druid Hills Presbyterian, on the following day.

Elise and Rich spent hours on the screened-in porch talking. They played gin rummy, listened to the radio, and played tennis at Piedmont Park. After one such match, he pointed to the weeping willow tree at the edge of the pond. "Remember that?" he said and winked.

Elise took Rich to meet Kitty and Harllee, and it increased her growing sense that Rich would fit into her family even though he was a Yankee. Harllee and Rich couldn't have been more different, but once they started talking war and fighter planes, they got on famously. Aunt Kitty told Elise "We approve!" without a mention of the relationship with Peter or their opinions as a comparison to Rich.

Rich told Elise that he'd been thinking about their future. Her heart skipped—to hear that, because he aroused new, deeper feelings in her. However, she was skittish about men coming on too strong, and she thought he was a little hasty in assuming a future together. She recalled how Peter had made her uncomfortable at first too, with his ardor.

Rich must have sensed her uneasiness, because he went on to say that he wanted to make sure that a future with him would not be risky for her and that he could offer everything she deserved. With that explanation, Mom relaxed and decided he was a fine man—responsible and thoughtful.

"I love you," he said. "With all my heart."

He kissed her. Elise said nothing and kissed him back. They held each other like neither wanted to let go.

"I love you, too," she whispered.

Rich invited Elise to accompany him to Ohio that November to meet his family. He would travel to Atlanta and they would go together by train to Cleveland—in Pullman cars with separate accommodations, of course.

The trip convinced Elise once and for all that Rich's intentions were serious—a man didn't take a girl to meet his parents otherwise. She worried about what to expect, but she was excited to meet his parents and travel north for the first time. Kitty had warned her that Ohio was cold and dreary.

Nana eagerly helped her gather up wool outfits and a fur jacket to prepare for the different November climate.

The day before Elise left for Ohio, she wrote a newsy letter to Peter. She did not mention the trip or anything about her confused feelings. She packed her bags, mailed the letter, and tried not to stew about her own cowardice. She dreaded admitting to Peter that she'd fallen in love with another man.

*   *   *

Both Elise and Rich were giddy with anticipation on their overnight ride to Cleveland. Rich talked and kidded, seemingly not the least bit nervous.

"You know, I should tell you that Mom doesn't know you're coming with me," he admitted. Elise was shocked, almost horrified, at the news.

"Rich, that's a terrible thing to do to your mother!" she exclaimed. "She will be mad as a hornet with you for not telling."

He shook his head. "Uncle Walter, my favorite, and Aunt Dorothy are picking us up. They're in on the gag. Our family is known for practical jokes on each other. Besides, it will be an even bigger surprise this way. I can't wait to see it myself."

Kitty was right: the northern Ohio sky was gray, the terrain flat. Dirty snow lined wet streets. Rich lit up as the train slowed and they neared the station. Elise kept expecting to see something beautiful in the scenery, but to no avail. Her stomach pitched, her mouth felt dry. The train jerked to a halt.

An attractive slender woman with wavy white hair and an equally handsome man greeted them. Uncle Walter and Aunt Dorothy hugged both of them and helped with the baggage. Uncle Walter and Aunt Dorothy had been unable to have children and they had always showered attention on Rich like he was their own. He, in turn, spent many weekends at their home in Chagrin Falls and loved being with them.

Uncle Walter beeped the horn as they pulled into the driveway of dad's boyhood home in Cleveland Heights. Lilly and Dick appeared out of nowhere before the car came to a halt. Lilly clasped her hands to her face and then back to her sides, clearly shocked but overjoyed—half laughing, half smiling once she grasped the circumstances. She jabbed her son.

"Elise, we are so happy to meet you. Rich mentions you in every letter," she said and held her arms out.

Lilly was a good six inches taller than Elise, big-boned and stout. Dick was also tall, with dark wavy hair and a stern face. Rich had explained that his father's poor hearing and general hardness made him standoffish.

Sis stood in the doorway and waved. She hugged Elise as she entered.

"Welcome, Elise. I'm Kathryn, Rich's sister. Please call me Sis like everyone else does." She let out an infectious laugh, just as Rich had described.

Everyone filed into the house. Aromas of succulent beef and apples filled the air. "Ma, you shouldn't have. Prime rib and apple pie?" asked Rich. Lilly nodded.

Lilly offered to show Elise to her room.

"Y'all are so kind to me," Elise said as everyone snickered.

Elise was flustered until she realized they were tickled by her accent.

To Elise's Southern taste, the dinner was good. But not great. The green beans were crunchy, the rolls were served cold, and there was no iced tea. Still, everyone was friendly and inquisitive about Atlanta and the South in general. She felt like an expert tour guide. Every once in a while, they asked her to repeat something. They couldn't seem to get past the accent. She thought they talked funny too. After a couple of hours she gained the nerve to tease them back, which they took in good fun. She especially thought they overworked their r's and k's.

Dad toured Mom all over Cleveland. She saw Case Institute where he had earned his engineering degree, and he took her to Lake Erie to prove it was impossible to see to the other side since Elise had never seen a lake that big.

"Isn't this something, Elise?" he exclaimed. It didn't occur to him that she wouldn't share his opinion or fascination with Cleveland. She thought it looked dirty and lacked style, but she didn't voice her opinion. It was winter—maybe everything looked different in better weather.

She noticed that people on the street rarely acknowledged each other with a "hello" or "good morning," but they would respond if you initiated conversation. She decided Midwesterners were just more private than she was used to.

Cloudy weather and near freezing temperatures put Elise's wardrobe to the test, but she took it in stride. Every once in a while, the sun broke through and made the surroundings more pleasant. And she says she was never more spoiled and regaled like a celebrity. Many relatives made special trips to meet the Southern belle who had captured Rich's attention. She thought all the people she met were polite and interesting—but she noticed that everyone worked hard and with seriousness.

"When do y'all have fun?" she said one night over dinner. It got a big laugh, but no one had a good comeback. There was no way they would have been able to comprehend her life in Atlanta.

Near the end of the five-day trip Rich said, "What would you like to do on our last night? I'd like to do something that you'd consider special."

"Dancing. Definitely dancing," she said without hesitation. "I brought a beautiful gown and my fur jacket. I'd love to give you an excuse to see it."

Rich pow-wowed with Sis in her bedroom, where she quickly attempted to teach him to dance. Elise heard music and Sis's hearty laughter. She suspected what was happening, but she said nothing.

Before the two left for the big night, unbeknownst to Elise, Rich phoned Nana and Pops to ask for their permission to marry. They were as shocked as they were pleased by such an old-fashioned gesture. "Oh, yes. Take her," Nana said.

Hotel Cleveland was the place to be seen in 1942. The fifteen-story limestone building sat on Public Square in the midst of what was referred to as "Cleveland's front door." The lobby featured marble floors, heavy columns leading to vaulted ceilings, cut-glass chandeliers, and a grand staircase of ornate turn-of-the-century gilded metal capped with a wooden balustrade.

A person could have a scrumptious meal there and dance to a big-name orchestra in a splendid setting. Rich had never been there before, which he finally confessed to Elise after they turned down several incorrect hallways, looking for the ballroom.

People turned and stared at the attractive pair: Rich, tall and slim in his dress whites, and Elise with her stunning outfit and glorious red hair.

Elise thought the food in such a fancy place would be different from Lilly's preparations, but the descriptions on the menu sounded the same. She said nothing about it and smiled as Dad ordered champagne.

"I'm not much of a drinker," she said. He said he wasn't either, but it was a special night. Elise didn't read anything into his words. Instead, she relaxed and savored the night: candlelight, music, being dressed up and with a handsome man . . . all of her favorite things.

She felt right at home in the opulent ballroom with its plush carpet and heavily draped windows.

Elise prodded Rich to dance, and he tentatively tested his new moves. Rich fared well, but he stiffened up from time to time, like he was counting steps or trying hard not to mash her feet. Once the orchestra tricked him by changing from a slow song to a jitterbug. Elise tried to keep him on the dance floor, but he said it was just too much for a guy who already had two left feet. They sipped their champagne and watched the more capable dancers. He seemed to enjoy it and commented on which couple he thought had the best moves, which tickled her. He clearly tried hard to enjoy her interest in an activity that was so strange for him.

"Do you think it's natural for a fellow to be a dancer?" he said.

Elise said she thought that it was something you grew up with, like a love of music. Rich agreed and told her that Lilly had always liked music and dancing, but his father had never really cared much about either.

"Maybe engineers don't make good dancers," he offered. "It would make sense, considering that we think primarily of function instead of beauty."

Near the end of the evening, Rich relayed how much his family liked her—that they were as taken with her as he was.

She smiled at his compliments. The whole trip had zipped by in a flash, and she had enjoyed herself a hundred times more than she had imagined.

"Elise, what is that ring you wear?" Rich asked.

She glanced down at her left hand. "It was a high school graduation present from my parents. The stone came from my grandfather's stick pin. Mother came up with the design and had a jeweler make it."

Rich asked to see it. She removed it and gave it to him. He inspected it from side to side and then put it in his lap. "Let me hold your hand," he said.

He entwined his fingers with hers. Without taking his eyes off of her he said, "Elise, this is for you," he said as he switched an engagement ring for the graduation ring and slipped it on her finger. "I can't say when we can marry because of the war, only that it is my intent."

Her eyes welled. "Can I kiss you with all these people around?" she said.

"Is that a yes? Because your parents already gave their permission."

"Yes!" She gaped in disbelief. He had planned everything. Rich grinned and told her that she would never regret her decision. He promised her a great life.

The band started up as the couple took the dance floor. Elise had her hand on Rich's shoulder. She watched the ring sparkle as they turned. She was engaged—again. And this time, her parents approved.

*   *   *

After several delays, Peter finally got approval for his leave in November. He phoned Elise to tell her he'd be home the next weekend.

Nana answered the phone. She paused when he asked to speak to Elise, but finally said, "Elise is out of town."

Peter tried to comprehend what that meant. She had never gone out of town and not told him. He was confused. He quizzed Nana, but she wouldn't say a thing except that Elise would be back on Thursday and that she'd give Elise a message to call him.

Peter mulled over all the possible reasons Elise would be out of town. Maybe she was sick or there was some new crisis with her daddy—the idea of another man never entered his mind. However, he worried because he didn't have a clue what was going on. They had always shared everything, or so he thought, so he knew something was not right. He decided to get to Atlanta that Thursday, even if he had to lie in order to move the leave up two days.

Peter phoned Elise the minute he arrived in Atlanta. Nana answered again, and told him Elise was resting. He insisted on speaking to Elise.

Elise answered as if drugged. "Peter, I was going to call you . . ."

"Is something wrong? Your mother said you were out of town. She sounded serious and wouldn't say where you were," Peter said.

There was a long pause. "I was in Ohio—"

"What in the world for? You don't know anyone there," Peter said.

"I'm engaged," Elise admitted. "To a navy man I met several months ago. I didn't think it was anything in the beginning. Just friends. But I do love him and Mother approves. I'll send back your ring and your pictures—"

"Don't bother!" he shouted as he hung up the phone.

Elise held the receiver with the dial tone buzzing in her ear. She bowed her head. What should have been a happy time took a sad turn. She replaced the receiver as if it were bruised.

Peter was distraught. He paced. He cursed. He drank. For two days he could not make any sense of the whole thing. He blamed Nana for undermining their love right from the get-go—she had never given him a chance in hell, never.

Peter decided to take matters in his own hands before it was too late. He drove to Elise's home to try to persuade her to change her mind. Elise's young niece and Nana answered the door. After Nana told Peter that Elise was at work, the youngster looked up at Peter and said, "Aunt Leesie doesn't love you any more. She loves Richard."

"So I've heard," he said as he turned and left.

The Southern Bell parking lot was not as full as normal. Peter parked the car and marched toward the reception area. His heart raced. He hadn't seen Elise in almost a year.

He convinced the receptionist to page Elise, citing an urgent matter to discuss with her. When Elise came through the "employees only" door she paled as soon as she saw him.

"Elise, we need to talk," he said as he took her by the hand into the stairwell. The door closed behind them. He cried. She cried.

"I'm so sorry. There was never a good time to tell you," she said.

"Elise, your mother is behind this whole thing. You must know that. I think you are confused. A Yankee? And a navy man to boot!"

He pulled her to him and held her tight. "I love you more than anyone can. Just get out of this thing, and we'll elope tomorrow. *We're* the ones who should be together. You know that."

Elise whimpered. "Okay. I'll do it. Somehow, I'll find a way."

Peter made her promise to call him that night after she fixed everything. He said they'd run away, if not that same night, then the next day. Time was of the essence.

"What have I done?" Elise cried after Peter left. Of course she had no intention of changing her plans. But Peter was so distraught, and she had just wanted him to leave. She knew he wouldn't take no for an answer, so she had lied in desperation. She felt ill with shame at her cowardice.

Later, Peter unpacked his duffel bag at home and waited by the phone. Finally, at ten o'clock that night he headed to bed. His stomach wrenched, his heart ached, and he felt alone for the first time in two years. Up until then everything had proceeded as he planned—he had his soul mate, the love of his life, the perfect woman and now she was gone. He cried some and felt worse.

By morning his anger had subsided, and he was calm again. Peter stared at the ceiling. "I'll love you forever," he whispered to the air, more from sorrow than loss.

Nana made no comment about Elise's bloodshot eyes at breakfast. She poured coffee and sat down at the table beside her.

"He found you yesterday?"

Elise nodded. "I think it's the right decision, but are you sure, Mother?"

Nana didn't miss a beat. "Absolutely. Rich is mature, responsible, and his family seems solid and worthy."

Elise felt tremendous relief that she had finally made a decision. She began to dream about her wedding. Her wedding to Rich.

*   *   *

Rich had warned Elise that he would only have about a week's notice for his next leave, the time at which they planned to marry. That meant a small wedding with immediate family and the few Atlanta friends able to respond on such short notice.

Elise and Nana shopped frantically for a dress. The one they selected fit perfectly. It was a soft ivory satin with a scalloped neck and embossed edging around the neckline that repeated at the hem and sleeve endings.

Druid Hills Presbyterian hosted the wedding ceremony. The red brick church with massive white double doors trimmed out in cream-colored limestone had only been built four years prior to the wedding. It still had that new look about it. A number of concrete steps created a grand entrance. Oak trees surrounded the church and were planted throughout the grounds.

January in most years would have meant freezing temperatures in the morning, warming to the forties by mid-day. But on the big day, January 23rd, 1943, it felt more like April. The weather had been so unseasonably warm for the previous ten days that the irises and daffodils made an early appearance. The surprised Ohio wedding guests arrived in Atlanta clad in wool coats and dark gabardines. Elise had advised Rich's family about what to bring and felt sorry for their flushed faces and sweaty brows. As much as she apologized for the discomfort, she took the weather as a good omen.

Simple bouquets adorned each pew and elaborate candelabra outlined the altar. The church organist played the Aeolian-Skinner two-thousand-pipe organ as if it were her last performance. Sun streamed through the stained glass windows and refracted light into colorful prisms.

Pops decided two days before the wedding that his skin graft disfigurement might dampen the festivities. So he asked his brother-in-law, Bipp, to fill in and give Elise away. As disappointed as Elise was, she understood.

The morning of the ceremony Rich delivered a long thin box to Elise's home—inside was a strand of graduated pearls, the perfect finish to her dress.

Rich pulled Elise in with his eyes as they said their vows, as if they were the only two people there. He repeated the words slowly, deliberately, and never took his eyes off her.

The reception was held at the Hunter home. The thirty or so guests meandered in and out of the intimate living and dining room and onto the screened in porch. A glorious day ended in a blur of warm greetings, hugs, best wishes, and pictures.

Bipp had his chauffeur drive Rich and Elise to the Biltmore Hotel downtown. Once they settled into their room, Rich helped her out of her gown. His fingers were warm and smooth. He kissed her and then carried her to the bed. All the fears she had about the wedding night disappeared. He took his time. He massaged her feet and moved up her legs. Soft kisses all the while. He waited to be sure. Elise lost herself in intense passion and then cried out, "That was wonderful."

Rich kissed her. "There's more where that came from."

*   *   *

Within months Elise became pregnant but she lost the baby. Almost a year later she was pregnant again. Although Rich was overjoyed with the news, Elise never felt worse. Morning sickness persisted way past the first trimester. She lost her appetite for almost everything except peanut butter and Saltine crackers. Rich was concerned about sufficient food for the baby as well as Elise getting her appetite back and enough rest. She complained about tired days and sleepless nights. When Rich was notified about going overseas, Elise returned to Atlanta and lived with Nana. Elise had wanted to be independent but relented when everyone agreed it was the most practical thing to do.

Rich wrote lengthy passages about the impending birth of his first child (which turned out to be me). He was as compassionate as he was curious. "What does it feel like?" he asked. "I know it's early, but I want to share in the sensations you notice. They say that women intuit much of what their baby feels, can that really happen? I can't believe how much is falling into place for us. Wow, I am one lucky guy to have the queen of all the women in the world as my wife. I can't wait to be with you and our baby when all of this is behind me. Please take care of your lovely self."

Elise could hardly bear it. They had been together for less time than they had been married when he was sent overseas and she returned to Atlanta.

Rich was not allowed to identify where he was stationed but he did mention heat, humidity, lots of showers, and problems with corrosion in his good watch. She imagined a horrible jungle, and it made her feel grateful to be in Atlanta amidst familiar surroundings and family even though she felt awful.

The baby was due in the spring. Since Elise had already experienced one miscarriage and persistent sickness, the doctor warned her against any exercise. The couple held their breath until she was in safe territory for a full-term pregnancy. In December Rich phoned Elise with positive news.

"I'm going to be sent to Elizabeth City, North Carolina, in February, and the baby can be born there. We'll have two months to get ready," he said.

Mom says she assumed she'd be having me in Atlanta. The subject had not come up for discussion because there hadn't been another option to consider.

"Elise, don't you worry," Rich said. "The navy doctors are the best in the world. One of the fellows told me a top notch OB/GYN from Boston is stationed there now. You'll be in good hands, not to mention I'll be there."

She thought about his remarks and decided that the Navy hospital, plus the doctor he mentioned, would be as good as what would be available in Atlanta. Plus, they'd be together when she gave birth.

Rich continued flying. A new problem had surfaced for him—airsickness. He wrote to her, "Today I feel like an old flat tire—positively and completely deflated. This airsickness wipes me out when it happens, and then lately, I haven't been able to eat afterwards. The instructor says this kind of thing is not so unusual and that eventually it will pass. The whole experience gives me a perspective on what you've been through with our little one."

In February 1945, the couple reunited in Atlanta. A very pregnant Elise and a proud Rich hugged each other around her stomach.

"My first baby," Rich said and patted her belly. It embarrassed her. Elise felt bulky and her back ached. She just wanted to have the baby and get her body back.

They stayed in Atlanta for two nights and then headed for Elizabeth City. Elise had always loved North Carolina and looked forward to setting up home there. She knew the town was on the ocean, which made her picture a great beach.

Rich smiled. "I hope you won't be disappointed. Some of the guys have told me what to expect. They say it's flat, as boring as any number of navy bases, and nothing to do. Maybe being on the ocean will help."

The navy men were right. The only bright spot in Elizabeth City was a new development where most of the servicemen rented modern furnished apartments. Yet Elise knew Rich would never go for that. It was too expensive, and he was a saver. Rich was always looking for a deal, which she appreciated but not always right away.

Elise scoured the newspaper and asked around town for other housing options. She panicked about not having more to choose from. "This is maybe the ugliest little place I have ever seen," she wrote to Nana.

Rich finally found a furnished second floor walk-up near the base at half the price of the new development where everyone else lived. The owner, a pig farmer and his wife, were seemingly right out of a storybook—sweet and thoughtful. The problem was the odor that wafted into the small apartment whenever the door remained open too long. Rich teased Elise about how stuffy the apartment was most of the time. She laughed along with him, but still she kept the door closed. Elise tried her best, painting the entire apartment and hanging curtains. In meager surroundings, but thankful to be together, they looked forward to their first child.

They bought used baby furniture that Rich sanded and refinished, a cradle that needed attention, and a high chair that was missing its tray. The repairs filled their night-time activities and everything looked brand new when they finished.

"What do you think the baby will be?" Rich asked routinely.

Elise said she didn't care as long as the child was healthy. Rich wanted a girl and said that he hoped she'd be just like "his Elise."

"Even if it's a girl, she could be like you," she responded. "Those things happen all the time."

On April 27, 1945, I was born. A little bit of drama happened just before delivery when a nurse left one of the side rails on Mom's bed down. She writhed in pain and was somewhat delirious. She rolled over and fell to the floor. The terrified nurse moved quickly. With the aid of a second nurse, they got her back into the bed and into delivery. No one said a word to the doctor about the incident, but Mom remembers that when she gave birth I was completely blue.

Mom cried. "Please tell me the baby is okay." Seconds passed like minutes before I screamed my lungs out.

That spring, everyone talked excitedly about the end of the war, but it dragged on without resolution. Rich was sent back to Pensacola in preparation for a new assignment. He finally got his wish and was accepted into fighter pilot training. Elise shuddered at the thought and returned to Atlanta with the baby (me) that summer. She says she prayed every night for it to be over before he had any missions.

Rich wrote about the excessive number of pilots who were in the program. He reasoned that being over prepared was better than not, should the conflict continue. He just wished he got more flight time. Without much to do, his squadron went sailing, fishing, or enjoyed other beach related activities around Pensacola. He said he felt guilty with his soft life, knowing Elise was busy on her own with a new baby and helping Nana with household duties. He wanted to be there to share the workload.

Elise figured Rich must be bored, because he started a list of requests about things he wanted her to do. He thought she should start constructing a household budget so they would be prepared once the war was over. She told him she had never had a budget before, but she agreed that it was a good idea. She didn't realize that in addition to the budget, he would require a report of where every penny was spent. It resulted in their first argument, by mail of course.

Within weeks Rich's daily letters indicated that he thought the end of the war was near. Elise got word that he'd be discharged on September 21, 1945. Rich planned to pick her and me up in Atlanta and then take us to Cleveland.

He wrote, "Mom and Dad have offered us the third floor suite in their home until we get settled. I'm sure housing will be as difficult there as it is everywhere else. Can't wait to see you and Nancy."

Lilly made the third floor look as much like an apartment, instead of a merely oversized bedroom, as she could. She used folding screens to isolate the bed from a sitting area with two comfortable chairs and a table. Still, it was trying. The north-facing window at one end provided the only natural light. The walls angled up to meet the ceiling and made the room long and skinny. The bedroom had its own bath, but it was three flights of stairs down to the basement washing machine where Mom did a load of diapers every day. Mom tried to be positive by saying she thought it would be a terrific way to get back in shape.

Dad admired how she accepted things and made the best of it. Rarely had he seen anything get her down.

Fall was a reasonable time to move to Ohio, with mild temperatures, crisp morning walks with me bundled in my carriage, and a bright palette of colors as maple trees dropped their leaves. Most people in the area were older, like Dick and Lilly, and a new baby drew attention. Somehow all the fuss was not enjoyable to me because Mom says I often scowled, which made people laugh. Grandpa Dick was one of the first who managed to make me giggle or smile, which delighted him to no end since many commented on his somber demeanor.

Mom and Dad read several books on child rearing before I was born and had agreed they didn't want to raise a spoiled child. The two main rules were to let me cry until I stopped before they'd pick me up and to keep me on an eating schedule. The first was hard on Dick and Lilly, who often snuck up on my bassinette and lifted me up into their arms for hugs and cooing.

Lilly cooked and taught Mom how at the same time. Her patience and good-natured attitude helped Mom enjoy learning a new skill. Then they would often stop to have a cup of tea. Mom says she'd never been a hot tea drinker until then. Lilly loved those breaks in the day with someone to talk to. They shared stories about their past and had many laughs.

"Rich wasn't always the responsible, conservative guy you see now," Lilly said. "He and his buddies were always up to no good. Nothing real bad, pranks mostly. His dad would get so angry," she said.

*   *   *

The more Elise was around Dick, the more she wondered if something specific had happened to create the family rift. Rich distanced himself from his father and there certainly was no warmth. Occasionally, Dick showed kindness to Lilly, but whenever Mom showed up with me, he lit up. He held me while he read his paper, took me for walks, or played with me on the carpet.

"Rich said he never saw his old man smile so much. It must have made him a remorseful," Mom said. "To say their relationship was tenuous only scratched the surface."

Dinner was a special family time. Lilly planned extensive and varied menus of pork, roasted chicken, and beef with all the trimmings. She paid great attention to table service and candles. Elise looked forward to the daily event as much as Lilly knocked herself out to spoil everyone.

Yet Dick rarely seemed to appreciate it. If Rich complimented Lilly too much Dick would give him a look that could curl spaghetti around a fork without a spoon.

Most Sunday afternoons, the young family rode the hours' drive to Walter's place in Chagrin Falls.

"Isn't it pretty out here, El?" Rich said almost every time they took the drive. Apparently he couldn't get enough of the country and his favorite aunt and uncle. He and Walter discussed plantings and the various animals that circulated through the small barn.

"No more chickens ever," Walter said. "The worst manure in the world, and then there's all that pecking. I'd rather pay double at the store for my eggs."

One day, after such an afternoon as they were headed back to Cleveland Rich said, "I should have been a veterinarian."

That shocked Elise. She thought his remark came out of nowhere. She encouraged him to elaborate.

"I've always loved two things: animals and medicine. It should have been my career," he sighed. "But when I shared that with Dad before college he had a fit. Said I was a second-generation engineer, going to Case. He told me there was no money or future being a vet."

They rode for a while before she asked a question. "You don't like being an engineer?"

"I'd rather have a job I did by myself . . . for myself."

Rich worked for Republic Steel for eight months. But when the union went out on strike, Rich answered a Franchester Farms ad in *The Cleveland Plain Dealer*. "Wanted: On-site manager for corporate owned 200-acre farm. Housing provided."

Elise could not believe it when he shared his news with her. "What in the world do you know about doing this?" she asked.

He said he knew a lot about machinery. Plus, Rich claimed he had learned from his Uncle Walter. He reminded her of all the weekends he spent as teenager and the many chores he volunteered to do.

She nodded. "But you were just a boy then."

Elise doubted there could have been anything of value on Walter's ten acres that would help a person learn how to farm. She worried about trading his income of engineering for farming. In the end, she decided that he must know what he was doing.

"Does your father know about this?" she finally asked him.

Rich shook his head. "I decided I wouldn't tell him until I see if I get the job."

Part V

Ohio/Atlanta 1966-1994

Between my junior and senior year of college, my best friend Joy and I planned to work at Shanty Creek Lodge, a resort in northern Michigan. Joy and I had clicked from the first day we met at Miami University. It was Joy who had discovered that each summer the resort hired fifteen college kids to waitress and tend bar. She promised that working and living away from home spelled adventure and cash.

When Dad died that spring, I assumed I would have to change my summer plans. But Mom encouraged me to go ahead with them, saying it would be good for me to get away from all the sadness at home.

"After all, finding help that drives machinery as well as you can't be that hard," Rich teased.

Rich's freshman year at Purdue ended as it had started—in disaster. He faced probation for his sophomore year. Mom took the news in stride and waited patiently for him to decide what he wanted her to do about the farm. I worried that Mom would have preferred me to stay at home that summer, but she insisted that she had all the help she needed, which I interpreted to mean Sally. The two of them always had the kind of intimacy in which they shared everything. Sally and Mom were both quite emotional, and their closeness also stemmed from Sally being the youngest child. I figured that if they had each other I wouldn't be drawn into the drama of things.

In contrast, Rich and I spent the majority of our childhood around Dad, who had avoided emotional displays. We had seen that as strength . . . Rich and I had both learned to suppress our tears. Twenty years after his death, Mom would tell us that Dad actually cried a lot, even though Rich and I saw it only three times: the soap box derby, John Kennedy's death, and the day the new buyer flew off with Dad's Cessna.

Rich and I were more apt to bond through problem-solving or debating the consequences of our choices. We didn't think the same on all matters, but I trusted him as he did me. Even if we disagreed later on in life over religion or marriage, at the end of the discussion we respected each other's point of view. Although nothing would ever sever our ties, when we talked about feelings, it was disguised in a joke or made light of. We guarded our independence and privacy, which probably made us appear insensitive to Mom and Sally, especially in the wake of Dad's death.

After I left for Michigan for what Rich called my "cake job," the stress of summer harvest and the rigor of cleaning the barns, along with the daily burden of milking the cows and repairing broken machinery, took its toll. Tempted as Rich had been to keep the farm running, after a couple of months he agreed that Mom should proceed with plans to sell it.

"I guess I only wanted a part of Dad with me," he said in his shy way. "But I know it isn't what he would choose for me."

The realtor warned Mom that it could take some time to sell. Dad had added almost too many improvements—three silos, two barns, calf pens, a milking parlor, two out buildings, an on-site generator, and a fence around the entire 126 acres.

As luck would have it, two weeks after Mom listed the farm for sale, a qualified buyer made an offer. His farm had been condemned in order to expand the interstate highway, and he wanted a replacement. He agreed to pay the asking price of $59,000, but he wanted to move quickly.

I was a few weeks into my job at Shanty Creek Lodge when Mom phoned with the news. She said Rich thought she should have an equipment auction separate from the sale. I agreed with Rich's advice, but it sounded like too much preparation to get done in a month.

"Should I come home for the sale?" I asked. Mom discouraged it.

"I think it will be chaotic and sad. I don't know which is worse," she said.

The tone in her voice caused me to change the subject. I rattled on about all the money I was making from tips and how much fun Joy and I had every day. I left out the part about getting drunk for the first time on Colt 45s, the unpredictable crying jags over Dad's death, and the heavy necking with a Troy Donahue look-alike that went on every Saturday night.

Joy and I lived with Gladys Carey, an older woman who'd rented us a room in her house for the summer. Living arrangements at the lodge were not included with our job. The day we found the "room for rent" sign we were ecstatic because the house was only half a mile from the lodge. Gladys talked to us at length before she finally showed us the second floor which had its own entrance.

"There's only one thing," Gladys said as we started back down the stairs. "You may have noticed a second bedroom at the end of the hall. That belongs to Jerry. You'll have to share the bathroom with him."

Joy's mouth dropped open. Gladys quickly added that Jerry worked nights so the bathroom shouldn't be a problem. I returned to "our" room with its twin beds, a large dresser, and matching nightstands. A braided rug covered the polished hardwood floor. I convinced Joy we should take it.

Gladys proved to be more mother figure than landlord. She let us use her kitchen each morning to make breakfast, and she lectured me about necking in *Troy's* Pontiac GTO. Apparently, she saw quite a bit when we parked in front of her house late at night. I assured her we only talked, but she was no dummy. I'm sure she thought we went "all the way," but it wasn't true. In those days, I was more afraid of getting pregnant than motivated to lose my virginity.

The summer of 1966 is still as magical to me today as it was then. Joy and I talked a lot about our mothers . . . how different we were from them, how we struggled to forge our own identities, how high their standards were, and how much we loved and resented them all at once. We cried over it, and with Joy's help, I began to feel myself hatching out of my shell.

We relished the freedom and our female bonding that summer. Joy became proficient at frosting my hair by using a bathing cap punched full of holes and a crochet hook. I taught her how to put in a Tampax . . . after a short demonstration, I stood outside the bathroom and offered support, laughing hysterically. She described what sex was like, but asserted that *Troy* was only interested in me because I was a virgin. It would be our only argument, even though I knew she was right.

Together, we explored northern Michigan's coastal towns of Petoskey, Charlevoix, and even Mackinac Island. Usually we met up with some of the other college kids at the tavern where we drank sloe gin fizzes and danced to the Shirelles. Somehow, we acclimated to the frigid Lake Michigan temperatures and swam every chance we got. Joy taught me to do a back flip, and I amused her with stories about the adventures Rich and I had on the farm. Her black sparkling eyes, dark curly hair, and olive complexion always provoked curiosity about her heritage—was she Greek? Italian? (Actually, Irish). I kidded that maybe I would have the same warm brown skin by the end of the summer. We were both five foot, six inches but Joy had a strong, athletic body whereas I was slender with skinny legs. We even kidded each other about the differences but mostly we wanted what we didn't have.

Spending the summer away from home with a close girlfriend was just the escape I needed to begin adjusting to the upheaval in my family life.

Meanwhile, Mom, Rich, and Sally moved into a rental house in Lodi after the sale of the farm. "I'll stay here a year so Sally can finish her last year of high school. After that, I want to buy a house in Medina. I've always liked the bigger size of the town and I'll finish out my teaching career," she said during one of our weekly phone calls. "Helen and Vennetta like the progressive things going on in the Medina school system."

In her very next letter, she included a photo of the rental house. I had pictured a bare-bones existence. What a surprise I had.

The temporary living quarters was nicer than our old farm house. A local builder had lovingly restored the place with modern bathrooms, a new kitchen with the latest appliances (even a dishwasher!), and a beautiful rock fireplace. He had planned to live there after all the improvements were completed, but his wife had changed her mind about living in the country. He figured that with a little time he could convince her to reconsider, so Mom offered to lease the house for a year.

"It worked out great for both of us," Mom said. "And Rich has enjoyed his summer job at the highway department as much as Sally likes her daily babysitting job."

I laughed. "What? No one misses milking the cows, the smell of manure, or broken machinery?"

In no time the magical summer at Shanty Creek ended and I begrudgingly returned to my "real life" and its challenges.

That fall, Rich returned to Purdue for his sophomore year, determined to prove himself. He mustered the courage to switch advisors.

Rich focused on his classes, and he received the necessary grades to be removed from probation. He never looked back, academically at least. Although his marks improved each semester, he longed to be back in Ohio surrounded by family and lifetime friends, even if the farm was gone.

I wish Dad could have seen the strength and determination of his son.

While Rich wrestled with his courses, I began my senior year at Miami University by student teaching in North College Hill, an affluent suburb of Cincinnati. The previous year, I had finally declared education as my major. Dad had tried to push me toward nursing or teaching for years.

"This country will always need nurses and teachers," he had argued. "You'll be able to find a job and take care of yourself if you lose a husband."

Whenever he had launched into this lecture, I reminded him that hospitals made me sick, and I was fired from my one and only babysitting job for spanking a rotten kid.

But Mom loved teaching, as did Helen and Vennetta. The three of them supported Dad's opinion and encouraged me to reconsider. When I chose education, they loaded me down with books and articles on the profession. I thought I had made a good decision.

The fifth graders who I taught in my rookie assignment were sons and daughters of college professors, doctors, and executives at Procter & Gamble. The school had full parental support and money—hardly the norm in the Ohio public school system.

Pat, the incredible woman I taught under, proved an excellent role model. I admired her strict and demanding nature in the classroom. She poured volumes of energy into the planning and execution of her lessons and expected nothing less from me. As much as the students whined about assignments I knew they appreciated and loved her. I vowed to emulate her style.

Rich and I talked frequently by phone about our post-college plans and where he wanted to live. Aunt Sis had connections in Cleveland and tried to convince him to interview with engineering firms there. She was disappointed when he rejected that idea, believing he would miss out on some great opportunities.

"When I graduate, I'm going back to Ohio, but I want to stay close to Medina. It's my home. And a part of who I am," Rich insisted.

I listened to him without comment. Everyone knew how much he had suffered from homesickness, even more so following Dad's death. After the first two years away at school, he had quit talking about it, but it still seemed to be right there below the surface.

"Medina, huh?" I said. "I dream of more exotic places to live—like Cleveland or Akron."

He chuckled. "You are a city girl. Besides, you never could tell the wheat from the oats."

Lilly visited Mom more frequently after Dad's death. She just couldn't shake her sadness and often repeated, "My only son, barely forty-nine."

As the end of her lease approached, Mom involved Lilly in her Medina house-hunting expeditions. The idea of Mom's move to new surroundings gave both of them a much-needed diversion.

"I'll like having you fifteen minutes closer to Cleveland, Elise," Lilly pointed out as if Mom had never noticed.

The women had different tastes, but they both fell for a compact ranch house in the Rolling Meadows neighborhood: its striking navy blue shutters, and Chinese-red front door drew their attention, and they were even more enamored with the mature landscaping framed by a crisp white fence. In the rear, a small lake enjoyed shared use by ten houses. Weeping willows dotted the banks here and there. Lilly liked the 'view of the lake' Mom would have from the kitchen as she prepared meals. I snickered over that when Mom told me because Lilly considered a kitchen the most important room in the house.

Harlan started dropping by occasionally to see how Mom was doing. Once, he brought a box of candy, somehow remembering her chocolate cravings. She didn't think a thing about it, but Alta and Vennetta jumped on the news like it was buried treasure.

"Elise, what are you doing? You haven't been a widow a year and already all this attention?" Vennetta said.

Mom explained that he was only being friendly and considerate—having been widowed himself.

Vennetta disagreed. "You better be careful."

Mom was upset over the criticism of Harlan and his possible motives. My instincts told me Alta and Vennetta might be right, but for some reason I kept my mouth shut. I believed once Mom figured it out she'd dismiss him.

I graduated from college in time to help with the move to Rolling Meadows. Harlan showed up to assist Mom, Sally, and me. He did the heavy lifting and offered advice when asked.

"Women can't move all of this stuff," he said. "Too bad Rich isn't home from college yet, we could have used him."

Actually, the move wasn't as difficult as I expected. Mom had discarded most of our tired, hand-me-down farm furniture. She'd kept a few nice antiques—such as the beautiful maple bedroom set from Lilly's Tudor house and an antique sideboard from Nana—but for the first time in her life, she splurged on new furnishings. While Mom worked with a decorator to select her sofas, side chairs, a small secretary, coffee tables, and a dining room set, I made plans for my first year of teaching elementary school not too far from Cleveland. The blue-collar area was heavily populated with Ford and General Motors assembly workers, and their children were considered difficult.

Even that pending challenge couldn't deter my newfound happiness. During the last two months of college, I had fallen in love. The object of my affection, Tom, was smart, athletic, attractive, and from a good Akron family. He came in the right package, and I was ready to get on with my own life. I remember bubbling over with the news to Mom. I embellished everything in the way a young lover does.

"He's just like Dad," I said, to prove his worth.

Mom tried hard to get to know Tom, the boyfriend who quickly became my fiancé. On occasion she alluded to his shortcomings: she thought him anti-social, self-centered and opinionated. I had heard such complaints from others but I defended him and kept the thing I loved most about him—the sex—to myself, thinking in my naïve way that it could cure everything.

"You should live with me Nancy. Until you get married," Mom said. "There's no sense renting an apartment when I have all of this room with Rich and Sally still in college."

I couldn't argue with her logic, so I moved in and anticipated my wedding day six months from then.

Harlan phoned every few days. Sometimes if Mom was shopping or still at school, I chatted with him. Once he said: "Tell Elise that I thought I'd plant her flowerbeds for her on Saturday. I think she could use my green thumb."

She took him up on his offer, still insisting that she thought of him as a friend when I kidded her.

Mom and I watched from inside the house as he labored all day in the yard. Mom offered to help, but he refused. Harlan didn't just mulch the soil and plant flowers. He edged the lawn, trimmed up the front shrubs, and re-landscaped the area around the back of the house. To top it off, he brought large pots for the patio that he filled with flax, ivy, geraniums and petunias. The changes made the house sparkle—Mom and I were both impressed.

A week later, I got home from a date with Tom to find Mom sitting in the rocking chair that Uncle Walter had given her when I was born. She stared out to the pond and rocked back and forth. Her eyes were wet.

"I'm so lonely," she admitted. She sat with a box of letters in her lap. Dad's letters. "These don't bring any relief, any more than all the other times I've pulled them out."

I removed the box from her lap and returned it to the back of her bedroom closet where I knew she kept it. I wondered what the letters said. Dad didn't seem like the type who would have spilled his guts or his heart. Some day I knew I'd have to read them.

When I returned to the family room, I knelt down in front of the rocker. I held her hands. Neither of us spoke. Her tears made me cry. She squeezed my hands and smiled.

"I hope you're that lucky . . . to have a man like him," she said.

Soon after that, Mom invited Harlan to dinner. At a minimum, she said it would give her an excuse to make a decent meal instead of leftover chicken or scrambled eggs. I was happy she had someone to share a meal with because I spent every possible night with Tom, who was due to leave for officer candidate school in the air force within weeks.

Mom told me they talked about their boys . . . Harlan's two sons still at home, as well as Rich.

They chatted about the future and laughed about life as middle-aged, single people. The evening went on later than either of them planned or than Mom thought she wanted. They made plans for the next weekend but Mom didn't divulge that to me until days later.

When Mom joined Vennetta and her husband for dinner at an Italian restaurant three weeks later, Elmer teased Mom about her "dates" with Harlan. Mom flushed, unable to see the humor in it. She cleared her throat a few times before she spoke. "There's no romance. It's not like I'm going to marry him or anything. We're just friends," she said.

Vennetta nudged Elmer as if to say "back off." She waved at a waiter so they could order cocktails and perhaps relieve the tension that threatened to spoil a nice evening.

Elmer ignored the hint and leaned forward. "Elise, men do not want to be friends with women."

Elmer locked eyes with Mom, who returned his stare in defiance.

Vennetta added a new twist to the discussion: "Does Rich's mom know about Harlan? She could be a bigger problem than the kids."

Mom sipped her water. She hadn't really considered what anyone would think of Harlan. She hadn't thought of him in the way they suggested. But, she realized then and there how the situation must look to everyone else. She remembered how jealous Sally was over the dates with Harlan even though she thought Sally would get over it.

Mom says her heart pounded the day she dialed Lilly's number to broach the subject of Harlan. She finally admitted, at least to herself, that a relationship was brewing.

"Lilly, I wanted you to know I've been seeing a nice man. Harlan. I'd like you to meet him."

The line was completely silent. Mom glanced at the clock. She pictured Lilly seated in her tidy apartment kitchen, smoothing out her apron as she digested the information.

"I see. Tell me about him." Lilly said.

Mom sighed in relief. "We met him years ago when he was on the FHA board," she said. Careful to make sure that Lilly knew the history, that it had been "we" not just her. Lilly seemed interested but she didn't pry with personal questions, like "Is it serious?" or "Do the kids like him?"

"Maybe you could invite Harlan for lunch the next time I'm down," Lilly said. "I could make your favorite: Welsh Rarebit and a nice fruit salad."

Mom smiled. "How I do love that recipe. I'm sure he would enjoy the meal as much as the company. He's heard a lot about you, I've bragged so."

"Oh, my stars. But thank you, Elise."

On the big day, Mom washed windows all morning. She vacuumed the whole house, dusted even though it wasn't necessary, washed the floor, and cleaned the bathrooms. Fresh daisies filled vases in the living room and in the bedroom where Lilly stayed.

"So you were nervous?" I jokingly asked Mom as she recalled the day many years after the fact.

She nodded. "More than if Nana were coming."

Lilly beeped her horn as she pulled in the driveway. She had always done that. She called it her "last-minute warning."

Mom ran outside and helped her carry in packages: raisin bread and coffee cake from Hough Bakery, fresh produce from a roadside stand, a tin of chocolate chip cookies, and fresh-squeezed orange juice. Staples, as Lilly saw it.

When Harlan arrived, he shook Lilly's hand with both of his. He told her what an honor it was to meet her and then he asked her questions about herself. He knew Cleveland well, having had several relatives migrate there. In particular, he knew a great deal about one of Lilly's all-time favorites—Hough Bakery. Harlan impressed Lilly with some inside gossip about the bakery that she seemed to enjoy as much as an episode of *General Hospital*.

Mom and Harlan praised the lunch—Lilly in turn, appreciated the attention and kudos. When she offered seconds, Harlan quickly accepted. The meal went off without a hitch—not a single awkward moment.

Afterwards, Harlan headed back to work at the VW dealership where he had recently taken a job as service manager. After a lifetime of manual labor, he had sold his farm and was anxious to learn a new trade.

Lilly helped Mom clean up the kitchen and engaged her in small talk about the kids and the weather. Eventually, the two moved out to the patio and stared out at the lake in silence.

"He's nice, Elise. A gentleman," Lilly finally said. "What shall I make us for dinner?"

My December, 1967 wedding went off with the predictability of a 60's Midwestern church ceremony: organ music for an opener, white bows on each pew, my family and friends on the left side and Tom's on the right, flowers and candles at the altar, "Here Comes the Bride" for my procession, and vows written by the staid and proper minister.

The only unusual aspect was Harlan's presence. He sat in the pew with Mom. They were later joined by Rich, who gave me away. Sally was maid of honor, so she avoided the unusual seating arrangement. It was a little awkward because many people didn't know Harlan. A few of my friends asked me if Mom was going to marry him.

"He's nice. They're just friends," I said, not at all convinced.

I wondered later if she thought about Dad as she sat there, the last one seated before the procession started. Was she sad? Did she worry? I thought about him but I never talked to her about it. I just couldn't.

Mom and Harlan saw each other regularly for a couple of months before she finally acknowledged they were dating. By then I was off, occupied with married life. Rich arrived home from Purdue and Sally from Findlay College for the summer, but they too were busy with their part-time jobs. Harlan talked to them with deliberate attention but never pressed conversation if it was unwanted. He gave them time and space to get used to the idea of his relationship with Mom. Sally held back, either disappearing whenever he was around or ignoring him. Rich, however, found a kindred spirit in Harlan, who was quiet, reserved, hard-working, and unassuming.

Rich was the first one to tell me about Harlan's diabetes. I had never known anyone with that disease and didn't know what impact it had on his health.

"You can manage pretty well for a while, but I think as you get older bigger problems can develop," Rich said.

"He looks strong," I added.

Rich explained that the disease didn't have a lot of visible symptoms but that diet was very important. I wondered if it bothered Mom or if she even considered being involved with another man who had health issues.

That summer, Harlan introduced Rich to his son Don, who was still in high school. Don had many of his father's traits: reserved and respectful, but also smart, athletic, social, and popular with his peers. Best of all, Don had no ego about his place on the totem pole of life. The five year age gap between Don and Rich had little impact on their friendship. Their bond was that of two natural brothers, something both boys needed.

"Don makes Rich laugh," Mom told Harlan one night after they finished a spaghetti dinner together. "It's music to my ears."

Both of them glanced out the window to see Don and Rich kidding with Dean, Harlan's ten-year-old son. The three boys monkeyed around on the dock at the pond. It looked like some sort of wager was being placed as each boy hurled a stone across the water. They laughed and slapped each other on the back.

Mom looked at Harlan and considered, for the first time, what kind of life she could make with him. She moved back to the sink and loaded the dishwasher.

"Sorry Sally didn't want to join us tonight. She made plans to meet some of her friends," Mom said.

Harlan nodded like someone who heard what was said, but didn't believe it. He said nothing.

Mom suggested a talk with Sally, but Harlan discouraged her. "I don't think it will do any good, Elise. Might even make matters worse. I'm okay with letting things be. She's lost right now."

Harlan wrapped his arm around Mom's waist and kissed her cheek. She felt the platonic affection one would feel toward a brother.

Mom phoned me in Illinois, where Tom and I lived near Rantoul AFB. She mentioned the increased dates with Harlan. It didn't alarm me but I still didn't take it seriously. He didn't seem like her type, not educated or sophisticated, even though I thought he was nice enough.

"Do you think it's more than dating?" I asked Rich on one of our phone calls before he went back to Purdue in the fall.

"Heck I don't know. But I like Harlan," he said.

Mom worried about what to do. Not just her life but if she should she should continue to see Harlan? How serious was the whole thing after all? Even though Alta and Vennetta asked her about it every other day, she said she hadn't figured it out. She told me in one of our phone conversations that she felt like she was just floating through her life. Neither affected nor inspired. Not loving or loved. She was simply on auto-pilot. No matter how much energy she expended, or the level of concern she had for an outcome, everything remained the same. Hollow.

I learned later that Alta asked Mom repeatedly what she saw in Harlan. When Mom said that he was a nice man, Alta waved her hand, "Not enough Elise."

Fall came before Elise was ready for the kids to return to college. She kept her head up as Rich and Sally packed, one day apart. Initially thinking it would be easier not to have them leave on the same day, she reconsidered as the time approached. As if going to the dentist's office over two days would be less painful than getting it done in one visit.

Kitty called two days after Mom had the house to herself. "Mother and I wondered if you'd like to come to Atlanta for a visit? Maybe Columbus Day weekend? It's my treat."

The invitation was warm sunshine on a cloudy day.

Mom hadn't said much to Nana or Kitty about Harlan, except that she had dinner with him now and then. Certainly she hadn't mentioned his two sons, the deep loneliness she felt, or her worry about the future. As her excitement mounted over the visit home, she realized how much she craved their opinions and advice.

Georgia turned on the sunshine, seemingly just for her. Never had she appreciated the landscape, flowers, and red soil as much as she did the day she arrived. She wondered how much to disclose about Harlan as she enjoyed the familiar views from the back seat of the taxi. When the driver turned onto Nancy Creek Road, Mom felt her pulse quicken. It had been more than a year since she'd seen Kitty, at Dad's funeral in Ohio.

"Hey! Lise," Kitty called out as Mom climbed out of the cab and hugged her older sister. Mom cried, unexpectedly, surprising herself at the outpouring of emotion.

"It's been hard, Kitty. Thank you so much for this," she said.

"There, there."

Nana appeared with hugs and kisses of her own. "Let's get you inside and have some iced tea. You must be exhausted."

Once inside, Mom relaxed. As much as she had always valued their opinions, she realized she'd changed. Conversation was easy. She no longer felt she had an image to maintain.

Kitty and Nana listened, waited on her, and reminisced over family stories. Never had she enjoyed the walk down memory lane more.

Afternoon naps were common in the household. On the first day, Elise spoiled herself with a nap. When she awoke she thought about her old flame, Peter, and wondered if he was still around town.

On the second day when the women disappeared to their bedrooms, Elise closed the library door and shakily dialed Peter's office, hoping he was still at the same number.

When Peter answered, she was so flustered that she hung up. He was taken aback but delighted to hear from her and to learn she was in Atlanta. He expressed sympathy about Rich's death, which he had heard of through Eugenia.

"Can I see you?" Peter said.

"Not at Kitty's. Maybe you could pick me up at the corner tomorrow and we'll have coffee," she said.

After they made their plans and hung up, she sat a while. She tried to picture him. She hadn't seen Peter since the shopping center run-in with Alta over eight years before. Hearing his voice made her ache to see him. So much had happened since they dated. Yet she also felt transported back to the same thoughts and longings she had when she was twenty. He'd known her when she felt more like a girl, and he was Southern. There were just things he understood.

The next day, a horn blared as she walked down the street to the corner. She turned to see Peter waving out his car window.

"Hey," he said as she climbed in. He leaned over and kissed her cheek, and she breathed in the familiar scent of Old Spice. She wanted to embrace him but refrained. His suit jacket pulled open as he sat back up, exposing a paunch.

"It's good to see you," she said as she tried not to stare at the change in his appearance.

He grabbed her hand and attempted to pull her across the seat next to him. She wanted to move but didn't budge.

"How are you? Still with Vivian?" she asked.

He kept his eyes on the road and made a sudden turn into the Westminster School parking lot. He shut off the motor and turned to face her.

"Lise, I can only guess at the reason for your question. But, yes, I am married. And I would never want to hurt her like you did me. Even though, in my heart, I love you as much as ever."

Mom dropped her head in shame. "I was only curious. I didn't mean anything like that, Peter."

He reached for her hand and squeezed it. "How are you? And the children?"

She glanced out the window. "We're all adjusting. I've been seeing someone that I think will ask me to marry him."

He shook his head and started the car. "It doesn't sound like you love him."

Mom fiddled with the collar on her blouse. "He's nice."

"You were the most important thing in the world to me at one time. You know that, don't you?" He wiped away a tear. Peter turned the car back toward Kitty's house.

They said quick good-byes. "Take care of your beautiful self," he said as he dropped Mom off at the foot of Kitty's steep driveway, knowing she would not want to be seen by her mother or sister. She watched him drive away until he was out of sight. She blew a kiss and started up the long hill.

Kitty busied herself in the kitchen as Mom entered the house through the back door. She immediately explained that she had gone for a walk even though Kitty made no inquiry as to her whereabouts.

"Can I help you make the tea?" Mom offered.

Kitty boiled water and got out her favorite beaded glass pitcher. "Elise, have you considered moving back to Georgia?"

Mom placed some lemons on the cutting board. "Right after the farm sale, I thought about it. I hardly got the first words out of my mouth before Rich and Sally voiced their objection. That took care of that. And now, there's another reason."

Kitty puzzled over her meaning. "Because you bought that little house?"

Mom shook her head. "I've been seeing someone. A gentle soul. Harlan is his name. I think he's going to ask me to marry him."

Kitty retrieved glasses and ice. "Oh, I see. That surprises me a little, but I don't know why it should. I'm sure it's lonely for you."

Mom went on to tell Kitty that she hadn't said anything about Harlan to their mother. She had denied a romantic relationship for so many months she didn't know how to bring it up.

Now that she had opened up to Kitty about Harlan, she felt ready to broach the topic with Nana.

It was a tense conversation. Nana shrugged her right shoulder as Mom explained how she and Harlan had met many years before, how they reconnected at the hospital and how helpful he had been at every tough turn. Nana didn't respond until Mom shared the last bit of news: that Harlan had two sons, ages ten and fifteen.

Nana started to leave the room. "Oh my, Leesie. He just wants a wife who'll raise his sons. What in the world are you thinking about at this point in your life? You're nearly fifty years old!"

Kitty interceded. "Mother, I think Leesie is capable of making her own decision." She looked away from Nana and smiled. "So tell me, Elise, what does Harlan look like?"

At first, Mom stalled. She so appreciated her sister's support. As she started to describe Harlan's physical characteristics: well-dressed, short, stocky—she wondered what exactly she could be attracted to. She decided not to mention the diabetes.

A few months later, Mom and Harlan married in a private ceremony, with each of their oldest children as witnesses. I remember a cold December day and strange vibrations. It certainly didn't feel joyous to me; it just felt weird. Mom had an odd combination of a smile and a frown on her face, and Harlan seemed nervous. The whole thing couldn't have lasted more than fifteen minutes. I think we gathered in the minister's office to sign the license as witnesses and then everyone disappeared.

Mom sat in the front seat of the car as Harlan loaded suitcases in the trunk of his Caprice for their honeymoon to Kentucky. She sighed and stared out the window, as if the answer to "What have I done?" would appear. She thought about Peter. Maybe romance and passion only happened when you were young. It was too late for speculation—she decided she would make the best of it.

"What should we call her?" Don and Dean asked Harlan privately when the newlyweds returned from their honeymoon.

Harlan pondered their question and told them they should make up their own minds. He said he was sure that Elise would respect whatever they chose.

The next day after dinner, Don moved to clear the table. "I'll get these for you, Mom," he said. Dean smiled and watched.

Elise was surprised. "That's very nice, Don. I'm honored."

"Well, shoot, you cooked."

Life fell into a predictable routine. Harlan sold his farm, and Elise sold the little ranch house. Each contributed equal money and they built a new house to accommodate their combined family in a beautiful Medina subdivision with lake frontage. It would be the only new house either of them had ever lived in, and they delighted in selecting the finishing touches for their two-story, white-frame colonial, including black shutters, a matching double front door, and a front porch with six white columns. Plus, living in town agreed with Elise, and Harlan came to like it, too. Without all the acreage of a farm, he was able to put energy into the yard, flowers, and a generous garden.

Mom continued to teach. She was in her thirteenth year when she volunteered to be part of an open classroom/team teacher program in a new elementary school that was designed with few walls and versatile open areas. The challenge energized and strengthened her talents.

Harlan remained a service manager at the VW car dealership, though he was not entirely happy there. His non-confrontational personality made him popular from the customer perspective but difficult from the dealership side. Harlan often sided with the customer. If a stern conversation was warranted, he became a bundle of nerves and froze. What's more, in order for the dealership to be reimbursed by the factory, or keep track of a habitual complainer, the job demanded a paper trail. Harlan's meticulous nature made it hard for him to complete all of his paperwork in an acceptable time frame to the owner. He turned his pent up frustration into his gardening.

"I always knew when Harlan had a problem at work because the lawn and flowers got more beautiful," Mom told me years later. "Come to think of it, we forever had the greenest and thickest lawn on the street."

Mom and Harlan made friends in the neighborhood and entertained. It seemed like each year when I visited, one of the neighbors dropped in for morning coffee or a glass of wine in the early evening. The household was usually bustling with kids, with both Don and Dean being talented and popular, and it teemed with even more noise and spirited challenges whenever Rich and Sally returned home for various vacations. A Ping-Pong table was set up in the basement, and a dock was built on the lake, where canoeing, paddle boats and swimming provided hours of entertainment. I thought all of the camaraderie was good for Mom and Harlan, but I suspected that the involvement of watching and helping each other's children grow up substituted for the lack of an intimate relationship. Initially I said nothing to Mom about what I saw, because I thought she had simply accepted this diminished form of marriage.

Everyone joined in the fun. Rich and Don shared a room, while Dean and Sally each had their own. Laughter over various bodily noises was common in Rich and Don's room, and the pair became the center of activity and jokes for the whole family.

Don had only been at Medina High School for one year when he was elected class president his senior year. His outstanding academic prowess and down-to-earth nature made him a role model for his peers and a favorite of all his teachers. Dean was also an outstanding student and gifted musically, though things came so easily to him that he had a tendency to slack off. Recognizing his talent, Mom prodded Dean to take on more difficult piano pieces and challenged him to add singing lessons. None of us knew what a fine voice he had until he landed the lead role in *Oklahoma* as a sophomore in high school. I still remember the chills it gave me as the curtain rose and a rich baritone voice resonated off stage with "Oh, What a Beautiful Morning." When Dean finally appeared on stage, a thunderous applause filled the auditorium. We were impressed and proud. Harlan cried and then later denied it.

"What a mother you are to my boys," Harlan marveled to Mom later that night as they put on their pajamas. "Do you think we could trade these twin beds for a queen?"

Mom pulled back the quilted bedspread of her bed as if she hadn't understood his request. "These are fine. And Harlan, they're good boys. It's easy. You deserve all the credit for the hard ground work."

He stood a minute and looked at her. With a big sigh, he moved toward his bed and, according to Mom, never brought up the sleeping arrangements again.

"Elise," he told her again weeks later, "you have a tenderness that we all needed. Because the boys lost their mother at such a critical time, I think they appreciate you even more."

His emotional revelation surprised her. Harlan rarely exposed his feelings, which bothered her. She was accustomed to a man who shared everything; despite Rich's outward emotional reserve, in private he had always been completely open with her—even if it was bad news, she preferred to know what was going on. But Harlan wasn't a talker, plain and simple, no matter what she tried. She accepted the difference but consequently kept her emotions and thoughts to herself. If necessary she talked with her friends, Sally, or me.

Harlan stayed at the dealership for eight years. As the years had passed, his discontent mushroomed. Out of the blue one day, he finally admitted to Mom that he wanted to pursue another career where he could be his own boss and work just for himself like he'd done on the farm.

"I've heard that before," Mom said. "Besides, you know it takes both of our incomes to make it."

Harlan quieted. He said he didn't mean for her to take up the slack, nor did he wish to be reminded that she made more money than he did.

Mom knew Harlan disliked the dealership owner, who Harlan claimed was cocky and condescending. She saw some of that in the man's demeanor, but there was something else. He was handsome—and—the spitting image of Peter and therefore she just couldn't help liking him, which she never shared with Harlan.

When Mom asked Harlan what he wanted to do instead, he said he thought he'd like to try selling houses as a real estate agent. This took Mom for a loop. She had to sit down on the edge of her bed to collect herself. She couldn't imagine him in sales for ten minutes. He was friendly and trustworthy, but it took more than that. The successful sales people she knew were aggressive, even pushy.

"I think you should stay at the dealership. It's a sure thing, Harlan. And right now, with our expenses and your boys still to put through college . . ." she trailed off as Harlan left the room without a word.

Tom was stationed at KI Sawyer AFB in Michigan for the end of his duty. We had been married three years by then. He rarely complained about the military experience, even though the Vietnam War was at its peak. He lamented over not having his sports teams (the Browns and the Indians) to watch and talked about the day when he would get his life (in Ohio) back. I taught school on the base while pursuing a master's degree in education at a nearby university. The constant distress of my students, whose fathers were being sent off to war, ground me to an emotional pulp. Almost every day, I cried as soon as I got home. The children taught me to be courageous with how they banded together, supported each other, and seemed to be able to accept their fate.

"Freddy's dad left today. Maybe you could read us an extra happy story," was a typical refrain from my brave students.

Tom hated the fact that I worked, and he saw little value in the advanced degree. He had hoped that I would get involved with the officers' wives activities. Nothing was more unappealing to me than that kind of life. We argued often, and things weren't getting better. Meanwhile, we drove back to Ohio each year for Christmas to be with our families for various traditional holiday festivities. The visit always proved stressful because Tom wanted to stay in Akron, with his family, while I traveled back and forth to Medina.

"I'm sure you'd rather go out there by yourself," he'd say.

Unhappiness began to overtake my normally optimistic frame of mind. I concluded that I had to end the marriage, and in the summer of 1972, I visited Mom to divulge my decision.

I don't think I was ever happier to be in her house than that week. The familiar scent of Estee Lauder perfume as she hugged me almost brought me to tears.

"I made fried chicken and apple crisp," she said.

We talked nonstop for two days about teaching, the neighbors, Lilly, the boys, Sally, Vennetta and Alta, and everything else. Everything except her husband and mine.

"What do the Atlanta relatives make of Harlan?" I finally asked Mom. I knew that Harlan had replaced her "girlfriends" in the trips to the South. She said they liked him. His desire to be the listener made him popular with everyone. He laughed easily, never voiced a contrary opinion, and was always willing to help with any kind of physical chore.

"He's so nice," she said.

I didn't have to think about her word choice. My opinion of Harlan was the same. I said that I believed a man should be nice. But it should be a given, rather than a quality worthy of points. Mom angered at my retort. In desperation I put my hands on her shoulders and turned her around to face me.

"Ma, are you happy?" I asked.

She burst into tears and collapsed into my arms. The two of us sat on the floor as I encouraged her to let it all out . . . her frustration and loneliness. I knew the answer when I asked the question, but I wasn't sure she did.

"Mom get out of this deal. There's no honor in staying stuck in a loveless marriage," I said. "I'm certainly not going to make that choice."

When I confessed my intention to divorce Tom, she expressed sadness but didn't seem startled. I finally revealed that not only had Tom fulfilled her assessments of him, he had added new shortcomings. He wanted me to quit teaching school, stay at home, have children, and he announced that he would be the ultimate decision-maker in financial matters.

Mom pulled herself together and told me that she understood my reasons for leaving Tom, but that she was fine with her life. Rich was happy, along with Don and Dean.

"To leave would be so selfish of me. And to not fulfill the commitment I made . . . I couldn't do that," she said.

Normally I would have taken her comment as thinly veiled criticism of me, but I no longer cared what she thought. My frustration in my own situation certainly matched hers.

I helped her to the couch.

"Are you sure you want to stay with Harlan?" I asked again. "What if this is how your life ends?"

She nodded and assured me she had considered that. "I had a love. In fact, I've had a full life. That's more than most people can say."

*   *   *

I prided myself on my Ohio upbringing, but I pushed at the walls that restricted my growth. Much as I loved aspects of the Midwest, I hated some of the attitudes—and the bad weather. I started planning a move before my divorce was even finalized in 1972.

Arizona—with its three hundred-plus days of sunshine and Wild West image—intrigued me. Tucson was smaller than Phoenix on the map, and I knew a pilot stationed at Davis Monthan AFB there. I packed up my VW bug with clothes and the set of Gorham sterling silver that I had saved for, and I headed west.

My five years of teaching experience and master's degree made it impossible to find a job in education, however, being that all of the schools I interviewed with wanted someone "cheaper." At first it discouraged me, but I rationalized that I wanted to make more money than teaching afforded anyhow. One morning as I drove east on one of the major streets, Broadway, I noticed a Xerox sign atop an office plaza. I made a quick U-turn.

The receptionist greeted me and invited me to have a seat when I asked, "Does Xerox ever hire women to be salesmen?"

She excused herself and hurried to find the manager. I hadn't expected such a warm welcome. She returned out of breath.

"They need to hire a woman by the end of the week," she whispered and then looked behind her like she wanted to be sure no one heard. "Affirmative action—your timing couldn't be better."

Ultimately, I became the first successful Xerox sales*woman* in Arizona. As the company grew at over 20 percent a year, the environment was competitive and difficult but financially rewarding. For a year of so, I was the only woman in sales amid fifty-six men, which thrilled me but confounded my mother. If she was proud of my pioneering, she never mentioned it, nor did she understand how I could be comfortable with so many men. Xerox would be the start of a glorious career for me in sales over the next thirty years and an appreciation of working almost exclusively with men. Men were easy for me—much easier than women.

*   *   *

An aging Nana retired to her bedroom in her late eighties, often spending weeks without descending to the first floor of Kitty's house. Nana's physical condition had deteriorated over the twenty years she'd lived with Kitty and Harllee, although she remained mentally alert.

Mom traveled to Atlanta twice a year to relieve Kitty and to give Nana pep talks. Sometimes she had time to see her good friends Eugenia and Louise. As much as she thought her trips were for her mother, she now acknowledges that she probably felt more refreshed than anyone else did when the visit ended because she escaped her dull marriage and life in Ohio.

If Harlan had enough vacation time, he accompanied Mom to Atlanta. He appreciated Kitty's gardens more than anyone ever had. He packed his grubby khakis and gloves and made good use of them.

"Oh Harlan, we could have had such beautiful flowers," Kitty said on one of his visits, to everyone's amusement.

Harlan didn't mind the work. In fact, he was more comfortable outside, whether it was in Kitty's garden or on some other project. The Buckhead lifestyle, however, left him ill at ease, although he enjoyed visiting Eugenia and Jimmie at their home. Mom says he relaxed and was more himself with them.

After several years of joining her on the visits, Harlan began staying in Medina whenever Mom traveled to Georgia. Maybe he sensed she preferred to go alone, but from my perspective, they both seemed to prefer the changed arrangement.

It was during one of Mom's absences that Harlan finally pursued his fascination with real estate. He enrolled in a course and began studying the material without telling Mom. Upon her return she didn't act surprised; instead, she supported his decision and asked which firm he liked.

"I haven't decided since I still need to finish the course and take the test. All of that will take a couple months," he said. "I'll stay at the dealership until it's completed."

Mom nodded. She still had her doubts, but saw no use in creating negative energy.

"I already have my first listing," he bragged matter-of-factly. "One of our best customers at the VW dealership, Mr. Warren. He told me a couple of weeks ago that he wished I sold houses because he wants to sell his big place out on Route 3 and move to Brecksville. It'll be a good listing."

In 1985, Nana passed away at age 96. Though she was frail in the last ten years of her life, her mind was as alert as ever. She maintained her love of reading and watching the occasional television program.

Mom said that two years before her death, Nana confessed that she felt guilty about her daughter ending up in Ohio.

"I feel responsible for your hard life, Elise." Nana shrugged her right shoulder and pulled a Kleenex from her sleeve.

Mom was shocked that Nana brought up the veiled reference to Peter. She wanted to ask her what the big objection to him had been, but she said she chickened out for some reason. Nana was obviously upset and it must have been hard for her to admit a mistake.

"Mother, it worked out fine," Mom assured her. "I feel blessed to have had the love I shared with Rich and the kids."

Nana nodded and dabbed at her eyes.

"Rich said he was going to make a woman out of me, and he surely did. I'm thankful to him every day for that," Mom said.

Elise, Harlan, and Sally drove to Atlanta for Nana's funeral. By taking turns with the driving, they arrived at Kitty's in one long day.

Traffic increased as they approached the city limits. Sally had taken her turn for last hundred miles because she had the best sense of direction and was unaffected by city traffic. Harlan dozed in the front seat.

"Wonder if Peter will come to the service?" Sally said in the rearview mirror to Mom.

Mom glared back at her. Harlan woke up when Sally spoke.

"Who's Peter?" Harlan asked and turned to Mom in the backseat.

Sally smirked like she knew an inside joke. "Harlan, you've never heard his name before? Mom's first boyfriend?" Harlan shook his head. Sally continued. "When Mom decided to marry Dad it broke Peter's heart. But, every year he called on her birthday. Dad thought it was hilarious."

Mom continued the glare.

"He hasn't called in a while, has he?" Sally said. Mom shook her head.

Harlan pulled a map out of glove compartment and studied it.

The chapel at Westview Cemetery was half full. The family sat in the balcony apart from the other mourners below. Dr. Elliott, who had married Mom and Dad years before, presided. As he took his place at the altar and began speaking in his rich, operatic voice, Mom's mind drifted. Dr. Elliott's kind words and slow pace soothed her ragged emotions. She rubbed her red-rimmed eyes.

She reflected on the number of family funerals she had attended. How many more would there be? And who would be left for her to lean on? Sally must have sensed a need because she reached over at that moment and squeezed Mom's hand.

After the burial, there was a reception in the church hall. Harlan moved to speak to Kitty as Peter approached Mom with his wife Vivian at his side. "We're so sorry Elise," he consoled her.

"It's always hard to lose your mother," Vivian said with wet eyes. "I lost mine when I was a girl."

Memories of earlier years flooded Mom's thoughts. She told me she wanted to rush into Peter's arms and leave with him. And never look back.

Sally appeared. "Hi, Peter, I'm Sally . . . Elise's youngest."

Vivian moved to speak with someone else. An awkward silence ensued.

Sally looked Peter up and down a couple of times, which caused him to flush. She didn't mean to embarrass him—she just wanted to check him out after all the years of curiosity about him.

"Sometimes I answered the phone when you called," she said.

Peter nodded and turned toward Mom. "It was a lovely service. Dr. Elliott always does a fine job. You take care of yourself, Elise. You'll be in our thoughts."

He turned to search out Vivian.

Mom couldn't believe that Sally had picked Peter out of the crowd. "How did you know it was him?"

"Are you kidding?" Sally said. "How about the way you two looked at each other? You heated up the airwaves."

Later, as the family drove out of the church parking lot, Harlan asked Mom if she had seen her old boyfriend. She nodded but stared out the window and longed for one more glance. She felt if she could just see Peter one last time she could endure anything.

After grieving the loss of Nana, Mom regained a positive attitude and life settled back into a flurry of social events, time spent with close friends, and the stimulation of her teaching career. When all of their children finished college and were off on their own, Mom and Harlan felt like they had received a raise; they finally had the money and opportunity to expand their horizons.

Harlan was curious about other parts of the world. He studied and prepared for each of the trips they took to Europe, Australia, Alaska, South

America and Hawaii. He enjoyed meeting people who were on the tours they took and he was an easy traveling companion. When they cruised to Alaska, Harlan resolved that he would learn to dance, which delighted Mom.

"I hadn't had a dancing partner in forever. It tickled me that he was so brave to tackle it. Especially at his age," Mom told me.

"Was he good?" I asked.

She hesitated. "He tried so hard and was such a good sport. Anything was better than sitting on the sidelines. Sometimes people on the ship changed partners, and then I really got to dance."

In addition to traveling the world and socializing in the neighborhood, the pair enjoyed their children and grandchildren (all of the "kids" were married now except me). The briefly quiet house at 337 Forest Meadows Drive filled with activity once again. Tricycles, puzzles, roller skates, and board games were crammed into any available cupboard space. A high chair became a permanent fixture at the kitchen table and a baby crib replaced the single bed in Dean's old room.

Lilly, by then in her early eighties, frequently drove to Medina. She enjoyed being around her great-grandchildren and often played games with them. Her days of taking charge of the kitchen the moment she arrived were over—she let Mom or Harlan cook. I teased her about it, and she laughed. She said she had learned that food tastes better when someone else makes it. Lilly was content to sit on the back patio with a view of the lake and tackle her crossword puzzle or quiz Harlan about the vegetable garden.

Lilly died in 1977 at the age of eighty-four. She was in Texas with her youngest daughter Peg's family, watching her grandson in a basketball game. The doctor later said that the excitement of the game, her weight, and age caused the fatal heart attack.

Once again Mom found herself at a funeral, contemplating her life's loves, come and gone. St. Paul's Episcopal Church in Cleveland Heights was a beautiful structure rich with history and warmth. The stained glass windows and aged dark pews gave it an Old World feel, much like a European cathedral. Sis gave a poignant and humorous tribute to her mother, which lifted spirits and gave way to the celebration of Lilly's full life and legacy: three children, six grandchildren, and four great-grandchildren, all of whom adored her.

Mom contemplated all that Lilly had done for her. From the outset, Lilly had been welcoming and cheerful, providing years of treats and laughter. Lilly had been supportive through all of the milestones in Mom's adult life:

the move to Ohio and later to the farm, remodeling the old house, raising three kids, Dad's funeral, the auction and sale of the farm, Mom's move to Medina, her marriage to Harlan, and Nana's death.

"I felt like I couldn't bear another family funeral," Mom told me after the service.

Mom dealt with the loss of Lilly by focusing on her students and her friendships with Helen, Vennetta, and Alta. Harlan busied himself with his new career, hosting open houses, showing clients around Medina, and once every leap year, selling a house. Despite his diligence and trustworthy personality, he never made more than six thousand dollars a year. It was a bitter disappointment to Mom.

In the early 1980's, I married Gary, a man whom Mom liked. Not only did she like him, but she also adored his mother.

"A man's relationship with his mother tells everything about his character and what he thinks about women in general," Mom said before my first marriage. She cited my Dad and Lilly as evidence.

Over the years, Mom's hypotheses weighed on me. Instead of an immediate dismissal, I began to consider the merit of her opinion.

"I can't believe how much you've learned over the last twenty years," I kidded.

"All I know is you've made a good pick. I'm glad that I won't have to worry about you any more," Mom said. She had questioned my taste in men on more than one occasion.

I laughed.

Gary and I had met at Xerox in 1979. We both sold a specialized line of machines that had engineering applications. Even though his territory was in Seattle and mine was in Phoenix, many of the west coast reps shared marketing ideas.

After a whirlwind ten-month romance that included summer boating and hiking Mt. Rainier, I agreed to move to his home in Seattle. One of my Xerox buddies in Phoenix claimed that I had no idea what I was getting myself into.

"It rains so much up there that moss grows on your ying-yang," he said.

After Gary and I married, Mom and Harlan visited us several times at our home in Kirkland, just outside Seattle. Harlan admired our waterfront house on Juanita Drive. Mom enjoyed the boat rides on Lake Washington, and Harlan pruned our extensive landscaping and fussed over my flower pots. We enjoyed each other's company and laughed at Gary's childhood stories.

"Do you think Mom's happy?" I asked Gary one night when we were finally alone.

He finished loading the dishwasher and looked over at me. "Elise is a happy person," he said. "And Harlan's a nice guy."

Gary was right . . . I hadn't thought of it in quite that way. Mom's positive attitude was a huge asset.

*   *   *

After thirty years of teaching, Mom retired in 1986, and was feted by relatives, friends, former students, fellow educators and neighbors. In fact, so many people wanted to celebrate with Mom that we decided to host the event on Rich's sixteen-acre property in Medina, where there would be plenty of room to mingle before the "roast" and buffet dinner.

"Elise would have quit sooner, but she didn't want anyone to know her age," Rich said to begin a humorous and touching toast. "Now Mom will have more time for dance lessons, roller skating, and aerobics. So much for babysitting grandchildren."

Retirement meant different activities for Mom. She returned to college for classes in art, music, and history. Sometimes Helen or Vennetta joined in. A new friend, Margaret, became part of the pack. I never knew teenage girls to laugh more than Mom's crowd. I was old enough now to sit back and appreciate the humor and wisdom in their stories.

The year after Mom retired, Helen had to be put in a nursing home. Her arthritis finally ended her mobility, and Alzheimer's had crept in. Mom said Helen didn't usually recognize her, but that didn't stop Vennetta, Alta, and Mom from continuing their visits. One of the last times Mom saw Helen, she was lucid.

"Elise, it's good to see you. This is such a bad way to end my life. I'm ready to go. I sure hope it's soon," Helen said.

Within weeks, Helen got her wish. Vennetta, Alta and Mom rode together to the service at the small Episcopal church in Medina where Helen had belonged for years. Mom told me it was one of the best funerals she ever attended. Helen had left instructions that she wanted everyone to have a good time filled with laughter; the minister even allowed the family to serve Helen's favorite drink, a black Russian, in the parlor after the service.

"Mom always said that Episcopalians were just Presbyterians who liked to drink," Helen's daughter joked to one of the appalled attendees.

When Harlan retired, he spent more time at Rich's place five miles away. Rich and his wife both worked and had three children. Harlan enjoyed working in their massive garden and doing other odd jobs around the property. He told Mom there weren't enough hours in the day to keep up the maintenance of the sixteen acres, let alone fulfill all of the family obligations and the restoration of the old farmhouse, which Rich insisted on doing himself.

"I don't know when the guy sleeps," Harlan told Mom.

"He is his father in so many ways," Mom said.

In 1988, Mom received an invitation to her 50th high school reunion in Atlanta. She had never attended any of the previous ones. She surmised that so much time had passed, it could be interesting. Her old high school friends, Louise and Emily, also wanted to attend.

"We can all stay at Emily's and go together. Just like old times," Louise said.

Ansley Park Country Club was the setting for the Girls High School class of '37 reunion. Louise found out that more than one hundred people from their graduation class of 350 planned to attend. Mom ransacked her closet for an up-to-date dress and accessories.

On the drive to the club, the three gossiped and admitted a bad case of jitters. They felt like freshmen all over again. Smartly dressed women in expensive cars jammed the parking lot. Not one woman looked familiar. Registration slowed the procession down. Mom eyed a brunette, thinking it was someone who had worked with Pops at the bank after high school.

"Elizabeth Collins?" Mom called out. The woman turned. "It *is* you! I'm, uh, I was Elise Hunter. Why, I'd recognize you anywhere."

The woman studied Mom. "Yes, I'm Elizabeth Collins, but I wouldn't recognize you anywhere at all."

Louise gasped at the rudeness. "What a snob. Don't pay any attention to her Elise. We're here to have fun."

The hostess welcomed everyone and asked that each woman stand, use their maiden name, and briefly tell a little about where they lived and their life so far. This quickly became a brag festival. Mom yawned as the afternoon dragged on. She wanted to loosen things up, and finally it was her turn.

"Elise Hunter. It's nice to be back with Southern ladies. I married and moved to Ohio, making me probably the only Yankee in the crowd." She paused and waited for laughter; none followed. "I taught school for thirty years and am now retired."

When she sat down, she stared at a sea of blank expressions. "I wished I could have buried myself under the carpet," Mom told me later.

The stiff affair worsened. It was a cross between an English tea and dinner at a prissy aunt's house. All three friends wanted it to be over.

Once away from the staid luncheon, the women fell into easy banter and enjoyed each other's company as much as they had when they were young. As in life, their conversation moved easily from the humorous to the serious. Each of them missed their mothers and worried about their husbands and children. They vowed to keep in touch and plan more visits together.

Mom planned to stay with Kitty for a few days before heading back to Ohio. The morning after the reunion, they lounged on the screened-in porch as Mom filled Kitty in on all the details. Kitty laughed as Elise recounted the funny episodes and pettiness, and she was mortified by the incident with Elizabeth.

When there was a lull in the conversation, Kitty asked, "Are you going to call Peter?"

Mom was stunned by her directness and that she obviously knew about the "secret" calls in the past. "Yes. I think so."

When Kitty disappeared for her daily nap, Mom dialed Peter's office number that she'd memorized years before. They talked for several minutes before Peter insisted on seeing her.

Mom ran upstairs to brush her teeth and put on fresh lipstick. She smoothed out her linen dress and pulled in her stomach. The thought of seeing him always gave her butterflies. She wanted to, yet she didn't want to. When she heard a car coming up the driveway, she hurried to the front door.

"Hey," she said.

"Hey yourself," he said. He hugged her and didn't let go. The familiar scent of Old Spice never smelled better.

When she stood back his weight shocked her at first. He was heavier than she'd ever seen him but he still had a full head of gray hair and was smartly dressed. She felt transported back in time with all of the same longings.

They headed to the garden, where they walked around some, exchanging pleasantries. Peter finally suggested a ride in his new car. Mom refused.

"I'd love to see your new car. But I don't think a ride with you is a good idea," she said.

Eventually, the two ambled toward the driveway as he grabbed her hand. Mom says it didn't seem possible that they'd known each other for almost fifty years. Peter pointed ahead. Elise looked up and saw what he had been so anxious for her to notice.

"Wow, a Mercedes. You've certainly arrived." She circled the car as if inspecting a blue-ribbon winner at the county fair. "I could never imagine having such a car."

"It's only money, Elise. Anyone can have this." He locked eyes with her. "Not at all what I really want."

After Peter left, Mom returned to the porch. She sat back in the oversized wicker chair and sighed. She nodded off briefly until two blue jays squawked over a nut. Mom watched them and cried.

"I shouldn't have called him. It will take me weeks to get over this and the whole thing is so pointless. So very pointless," she thought.

Harlan's diabetes eventually caught up with him. He began having blackouts and unpredictable chemical imbalances that he could not control with insulin. Soon, the fear of driving his car or even leaving the house consumed him. Depression replaced his cheerful disposition, and he sat in the La-Z-Boy for hours staring out at the lake.

Elise conferred with doctors, his children, and their pastor. Everyone decided that a change of scenery for the winter would be good, not to mention the warmth and ocean that Florida offered. Elise planned a vacation in 1993 to Siesta Key, one of Harlan's favorite destinations, and he seemed to perk up at the news.

Mom read him the weather forecast and described activities she thought he'd like once they arrived. "We can go to the Sailor's Circus, walk on that old beach out on Longboat Key where you always find interesting shells, and we can go to the Oyster Bar on Friday night."

Harlan spirits rallied for a while.

"I don't think I can help you drive, Elise," he said with a sad face.

Mom laughed. "That's okay. We'll get there faster if I drive."

The sunny January weather in Florida was fifty degrees warmer than what they left behind in Ohio. Harlan relaxed, soaked in the hot tub, and sometimes joined Elise for strolls on the white sandy beach. His mood improved tenfold.

The third week of their vacation, Harlan decided to sit in a beach chair while Mom waded through the waves to a bulkhead some distance away. When she returned an hour later, Harlan had not moved an inch. She waved to him as she approached.

"Sorry I was gone so long. There was a school of porpoise close to shore," she said.

Harlan stared at her without response.

Mom knelt in front of him. "Harlan, are you alright?"

His head didn't move, he had no expression, and his eyes were glassed over.

Elise took his hand. "Harlan, can you tell me what's wrong?"

No response. A passerby stopped. "Can I help?" the man said.

Mom nodded. "My husband's a diabetic. He wasn't hungry earlier, but he should have had lunch an hour ago. Please, could you call an ambulance?"

The man hurried off. "Stay right here," he yelled.

Elise pulled a piece of candy out of her pocket and tried to put it in Harlan's mouth. It fell to the sand.

The paramedics ran toward the beach armed with oxygen and a medic kit. People cleared a path and stood helpless as the crew leader inspected Harlan. He shined a light into his eyes.

"Can you feel this?" the young man asked as he squeezed Harlan's hands. There was no response.

"Even though his eyes are open, he isn't conscious. He's had a stroke," the paramedic said as the crew hustled a gurney beside the beach chair.

"Are you sure?" Mom asked. "He's had diabetic comas before. It looks the same as this, as I recall."

"It could be both, ma'am. We'll take him to Florida General. You come with us."

*   *   *

The doctors concluded it was an unusual stroke that had occurred in the deepest part of the brain controlling consciousness. They explained that the stroke might have been triggered by a diabetic coma. The prognosis was not encouraging: Harlan would need to stay in the hospital a couple of weeks to be stabilized and then he would require therapy to regain mobility, speech, and continence.

Mom cried. "This is all my fault. If I had insisted he have lunch before we went to the beach, none of this would have happened."

The doctor comforted her. "Not true. He has managed his diabetes for years, but this is the downside of the disease. Diabetics are more prone to strokes."

Elise stayed at Harlan's bedside and dozed in a chair. She did not want him to wake up alone since the doctors claimed he would have no recollection of what happened. A few hours after Harlan was admitted, he awoke, groggy and confused.

"Leeeeese. Wha happppen?"

She took his hand and explained, which seemed to calm him. He motioned for water. Mom propped him up and held the glass for him to sip. He got some in his mouth and dribbled some down his chest.

"You're lucky, Harlan. No paralysis," she said. "The doctor should be back to check on you early this evening. He said you'd need to stay for a couple of weeks until you regain certain motor skills. Then some therapy."

"Wan to lay don." He dozed almost immediately.

Harlan regained his speech within days, though it was slow and deliberate. All of his other motor skills returned too, except continence. The doctor warned that if it didn't return soon, he'd need to have a catheter inserted. Harlan hated that threat, but the embarrassment of having Mom clean him up was much worse.

Mom hoped that when they returned to Medina, Harlan would have success in regaining control of his bladder. She believed less stress could prevent an accident. Hope replaced reason as both of them wrestled with the devastating change.

The doctor counseled Mom. "If the duration of a stroke is brief, or if the muscles can be exercised soon afterward, it will allow the brain cells that control bladder function to rejuvenate. However, the more time passes, the worse the situation. Damaged brain cells cannot be repaired or replaced," he said. "I'm afraid that Harlan suffered the worse alternative."

"What if he uses the toilet on a regular basis? Say, every hour?" Elise asked.

The doctor looked doubtful. "You could get lucky, but that's all it would be. Whether Harlan is in the bathroom or not, he can't control or influence what happens."

There were no more questions. Mom stepped out of the exam room for the doctor to insert the catheter.

It was a long ride back to Ohio. No talk, no radio, no smiles. Nothing.

"For better or for worse," Mom reminded herself. No one ever really thinks about the "worse" or believes it will happen. She felt sorry for Harlan but she knew any words to that effect would only make him more uncomfortable.

After the first bad accident, Elise cleaned Harlan up like you would a baby. She used a washcloth, mild soap, and talcum powder. He cried.

"It's okay, Harlan. I'll take care of you. Don't you go feeling sorry for yourself, *we* will deal with it," Mom said.

Harlan pulled himself together. The next day he told her he wanted to get his affairs in order. "I want to make sure the living will is still valid and enforceable."

Mom nodded. She knew this was a wise course of action.

Harlan never cried again. He simply quieted more than usual. Nothing held his interest: not food, television, his children, or sports. He folded in on himself and withered. Slowly, at first.

*   *   *

Eugenia called Elise every few months, or vice versa.

"The sound of her voice always picked me up, no matter how bad things were," Mom told me.

Sometimes Jimmie got on the phone. He told her that old friends needed to stick together and that she could count on them for their support. Elise thought more and more about Atlanta after each phone call. It made her homesick.

In January 1994, Eugenia phoned to tell Mom that Vivian had died after a brief but severe bout with cancer. She gave Mom Peter's home number and encouraged her to call him.

Recently, Mom told me that she thought about it for a week. She started to dial several times and hung up.

"Were you scared or nervous?" I asked.

She shrugged like she didn't know which one. She said that when they finally did talk, Peter told her how much he appreciated her call and condolences. Mom told him about Harlan's ill health.

"I'd like to talk to you again," Peter said. Mom hesitated but gave him her number.

It was a lot to deal with: diabetes, incontinence, and steady slippage of the mind. A year after the stroke, Harlan took a turn for the worse and was admitted to a nursing home. Harlan's children stepped forward to ease the financial burden and arranged to take turns staying with him to help his morale.

"Dad's always been a fighter," the oldest son said.

Mom didn't comment. She knew he was too young to fully grasp what it felt like to lose your quality of life. It was impossible to explain to the children that their father would never be better—they were in denial about the gravity of his condition. She alone knew that Harlan would never leave the nursing home.

An even further turn for the worse sent Harlan to the intensive care ward of the hospital, where he received a higher dosage of pain medication.

The children objected to the living will Harlan signed and insisted that everything be done to keep him alive. But Harlan had pain that medication couldn't touch. Mom fretted but she didn't know where to turn.

"Please. Please, make them understand," were Harlan's last words to her.

With the help of the doctors and their minister, the children finally accepted his condition and their impending loss. Harlan slipped into a coma.

"You are a good man, Harlan," Mom said softly and stroked his hand. "I'm sorry it wasn't more of a marriage. Thank you for always being so thoughtful and kind to me and my kids. Thank you."

Harlan lay motionless and pale for two days. The family hovered around his bed all hours of the day.

"God bless you," Mom whispered the last time she spoke to him. She kissed his hand.

A tear formed in the corner of Harlan's left eye and ran down his cheek.

After Harlan passed away, Mom dealt with all of the paperwork and arrangements as if in a fog. She drove herself home from the hospital, pulled into the garage, and sat there stunned, glancing at all the clutter of twenty-five years of marriage: garden tools, toys for grandchildren, an extra refrigerator and freezer, boxes of Christmas decorations, odd pieces of luggage, and Harlan's old car that Rich and Don had nicknamed the "green latrine."

"I need to clean house," she thought. "But where to start?"

She leaned her head down on the steering wheel. She felt beyond crying, and it scared her. She thought about her past loves, the fulfilled commitment of the marriage to Harlan, the sacrifices . . . and now she had a life just for herself. The whole idea of living for herself, by herself, seemed strange.

"I can do this," she said. "I think I can do this."

Part VI

Ohio/Georgia 1994-1995

The last years of Harlan's life aged my mother, and I worried about how exhausted she sounded after the ordeal of his illness and death. I tried to imagine what it would feel like to outlive two husbands. What kind of life awaited a seventy-five-year-old widow? How well would Mom handle living on her own for the first time?

While I pondered these questions and fretted afar from Seattle, the rest of the family rallied to help Mom move into the next phase of her life. Rich and Don volunteered to clean out the garage for a sale. They scoffed at Mom's idea to simply give away the tools, lawn maintenance items, and piles of other supplies.

"There's probably two thousand dollars worth of equipment out there," Don told her. "Whatever we can't sell, you can donate."

After the garage sale, they cleaned out the basement, the attic, and tackled the list of minor repairs that needed to be done before the "too big" house could be put on the market. Rich reported on the progress, which I appreciated, but I felt guilty about not being there to lend a hand.

"I could come home to help," I said to Mom as I paced around my kitchen on the portable phone.

"Oh no," she said. "It's such a long trip for you from Seattle. Besides, I think I'll go ahead with buying that condo I told you about."

The week before she had sent photos of the Presidents' Row complex five blocks from the house she'd shared with Harlan. The unit she selected was a third the size of the house but it offered an efficient floor plan with attractive finishes. Rich added that his firm had done all of the civil engineering work on the project and that the builder had a good reputation.

"Maybe you'd come and help me decorate after I get moved in?" Mom suggested. I smiled, grateful to hear her upbeat and hopeful tone, and I realized how much I missed her.

Though Mom and I had become helpful and open to each other in recent years, our relationship had not always been harmonious. We battled more frequently in the decade after my divorce from Tom, when I settled in Arizona and embarked on my hard-charging career. Mom's strong opinions seemed to deepen then, as did my stubbornness, while we attempted to find common ground as adults. We definitely didn't want the same things in life. She believed my generation had a bad case of the "me-me-me's," and I thought she aspired to martyrdom. I had material aspirations, and she sought solace in religion.

"Marriage is a commitment—not a wedding day. Your generation gives up easy," she claimed.

Whenever she vocalized her displeasure over my taste in men, I resisted her criticism. Even when she was right. When I married Gary, whom she adored, our debates began to diminish. The angst of our differences slowly faded as we forged a new-found respect for each other.

In recent years, we had settled into a routine: I visited Ohio once a year and she occasionally came to see me by herself in Seattle. We tried to take advantage of weather to increase the pleasure. She loved being on Lake Washington. She insisted on going to my aerobics class and meeting my clients and working pals, as well as cooking her famous fried chicken and cheese grits for our friends. Her curiosity about my life was as refreshing as it was enjoyable.

In turn, she began to tell me things about her life: memories of her childhood, how much she missed Georgia and why, all the fun she had as a girl, the depth of her relationship with Nana, and just how much she loved teaching. I finally had the time—and interest—to listen. My questions spurred her into further reflections and insights, without any of the conflict that had infused our conversations when I was younger. Perhaps the change in our relationship enabled her to trust me with more.

The week before Mom was to close on the condo she decided to take a spur-of-the-moment trip to Atlanta. I thought she simply missed Kitty or perhaps her Atlanta friends. I didn't consider that she might be having second thoughts about staying in Medina.

It was late fall when Mom traveled South by herself. The weather in Ohio had already taken on a winter chill, while the temperatures in Georgia remained moderate. As she rode in the taxi from the airport, she thought about the differences in the climate, the scenery, the daily life. She wondered what it would be like to live there again . . . if she could. Everyone always said things about how "you can never go back home." She still had her old friendships with Jimmie, Eugenia, and Louise, even though they were married and now she wasn't.

Kitty outdid herself with plans that included a special Sunday service at Druid Hills Presbyterian Church. Mat brought Mom breakfast in bed and reminisced with her over funny stories about Nana.

The second day, Mom and Kitty shopped and then later sat in the living room and read. Kitty finally announced that she was going upstairs for her nap. She winked at Mom and left.

Mom said she sat there for a bit and looked out the window. She closed the book she was reading and walked toward the library. Once inside, she stood with her hand on the door knob and stared at the phone on the desk.

"Five minutes I stood there, at least," she told me a few years ago.

"Finally, I closed the door and went upstairs for a nap myself."

She enjoyed the next five days with Kitty and then returned to Medina. She made no phone calls.

*   *   *

Mom unpacked boxes in her new condominium as Vennetta and Alta laughed over many silly things and debated on which cabinets to use for glassware, plates, and spices. The pair had been by Elise's side through the home sale, the move, and as she settled into the condo. Margaret stopped in from time to time with special treats. Everyone agreed she had a chocolate thumb when it came to baking fabulous desserts.

Margaret had joined the group just two years before. She was ten years younger than the others and full of vinegar because her high-profile husband had dumped her for a much younger woman. Margaret would get alimony for the next twenty years, so she at least didn't have to worry about finances.

Still, I wondered why Margaret didn't want to get a job just to have something to do, let alone be in an environment where she might meet men. I had noticed the couple of times I'd been around Margaret that she made humorous quips about how much she missed a man's pair of slippers under her bed.

"Just for a night," she said once. "Okay, maybe the weekend."

Mom and Vennetta usually laughed. If Alta was around, she might smirk or simply not respond.

"How come Alta doesn't like Margaret?" I asked Mom, after witnessing their dynamic on one of my visits. "Alta typically likes a spunky personality."

Mom explained that Alta was jealous and worried about losing a friend—herself—that she'd had for over forty years. "Alta can be possessive," she added.

I called Mom the first night she moved into the condo. She sounded exhausted, but she assured me she was receiving tons of support from Rich, Don, and her girlfriends. Yet there was something strange in her voice that I had never heard before. It nagged at me for hours after we ended our conversation. Was it relief or sadness? One thing I knew for sure, she didn't sound chipper.

I voiced my concern when I spoke to Rich the next day, but he discounted my fears. "She's fine. It was a long day. She's no spring chicken, you know."

It was typical of Rich to miss subtle changes. Even though what he said about Mom was true, I knew her to be positive at all costs and had never heard her sound defeated for so long. I decided to call her every day for a while and see if her mood improved.

Several days passed, and I believed that she sounded better. I made plans to travel to Medina right before Thanksgiving to help Mom decorate the condo for the holiday. Mom wanted to host Rich's family for the big day, and she said that there were still things to buy here and pictures to be hung.

When I arrived, I was pleasantly surprised by all of the work she'd done since moving in a month earlier. New furniture in the living room and dining room created an inviting, lived-in effect. The off-white, peach and tan colors lent the rooms a spacious and airy feel.

"What in the world is left to do?" I said.

"Stools for the breakfast bar and hang a few pictures. Plus, I really wanted to talk to you. Just you."

This news puzzled me. Mom and Sally were the closest.

"I've been talking to someone special for the last week," she said in a nervous school-girl kind of voice.

I had learned first hand how much Mom didn't like being alone. Her tone alarmed me. "Oh no, not another guy!"

She cleared her throat. "No, well . . . yes. But not just any guy. Peter."

The name came out of left field; I recognized it, but I hadn't thought of him in a long while. "Georgia Peter? Your old beau?"

"Yes."

That opened the door for a million questions, which she rushed to answer with excitement and breathless energy. She explained that she had learned of Vivian's death earlier that year, in January, from Eugenia and called Peter to express her condolences. Peter was glad to hear from her. They had a brief but sweet conversation, and when Peter asked if he could have her phone number, Mom gave it to him.

"And then Peter called you again?"

"Once," she said. "When Harlan went into the nursing home and then not again until he learned from Eugenia that Harlan had died."

I poured myself a big glass of wine even though it wasn't cocktail time, and encouraged her to continue.

"Wow," I said. "So what are your plans?"

She said that it was good to reconnect with such an old friend, someone that she had such fond memories of. She claimed there weren't plans of any kind.

*   *   *

When I visited in Atlanta in 2003, Eugenia and Jimmie invited me to have lunch with them at their favorite place, Eastlake Country Club. We sat at a window table in the Bobby Jones room. Normally, it would have been their day of the week to play nine holes together and then have lunch, but the chilly fall morning and Eugenia's arthritic knee altered their usual plan. She encouraged Jimmie to play with his pals and meet up with us later. That would give us more time to catch up and for her to fill me in on some of her recollections of the past.

A waiter brought a basket of assorted muffins and filled our water glasses. Eugenia leaned forward and surveyed the choices. I sat back and enjoyed her humorous observations.

"You and Mom have been friends for over fifty years, right?" I confirmed.

Eugenia's bright eyes danced as she nodded.

"Where does the time go? We have had so many good times and wonderful memories," she said.

We had hardly caught up on all the changes in our lives when Jimmie strolled in with a wave to us.

"How'd you do today, darlin'?" she said.

Jimmie gave her one of his "aw shucks" grins. "The golf gods were with me today. I shot a forty-two. Not bad for an old guy."

"Wonderful! Bet you won all the money," she said. "I was just filling in Nancy about the phone calls Elise got from Peter after Harlan died, do you remember that?"

Jimmie nodded in a knowing sort of way. "As I recall, we both thought it would be just a matter of time."

Eugenia stirred her coffee and glanced at the lunch specials on the menu. She peered over the top of her reading glasses. "I think my exact words were 'wonder what will happen now.'"

*   *   *

Peter began to call daily. Mom said they talked about everything: families, gardening, cooking, old friends, their health, and their past relationship. She looked forward to the calls more than she ever imagined she would. For the first several weeks she told me—and only me—about the phone calls. She must have worried about Sally being jealous of Peter.

Her mood took a monumental leap. She giggled all the time. She shared her thoughts, and she wanted to discuss her clothes, keeping fit, what diet worked fastest, who had the best makeup nowadays, and what books I was reading. Old lady conversations full of nothing but grandchildren and the weather had been sidelined. She was back among the living.

"When are you going back to Atlanta?" I asked her just before Thanksgiving.

She didn't hesitate. "The day after turkey day . . . if I can convince Vennetta and Margaret to drive down with me."

I teased her that she had told me there were "no plans of any kind." When she didn't react to my sarcasm, I told her that she didn't need chaperones to see Peter, unless she was scared.

"Oh I'm scared all right," she said. "It's been over fifty years since we were involved. Things change."

Initially, Mom used the excuse of wanting to see Kitty and Harllee's new retirement home when she invited Vennetta and Margaret to drive with her to Atlanta. Before the travel plans were finalized, Mom admitted that she had talked to Peter and that he invited all of them to stay at his house. The three agreed that staying at a hotel would be more comfortable. Margaret said to tell Peter that he could still cook for them even if they weren't staying with him.

Mom said that Vennetta and Margaret teased her to no end during the whole trip. She claimed not to mind, but I was skeptical—Mom only endures teasing for limited amounts of time.

It was early afternoon when the threesome pulled into the Terrace Garden Hotel on Lenox Road. After a quick check-in, Mom dialed Peter's number.

Margaret smirked. "You calling Kitty?"

Peter answered on the first ring and said he'd be right over.

Mom said she felt dizzy. Her two friends seemed to delight in watching her discomfort as she wondered what *right over* meant. Five minutes or fifteen? Mom was as nervous as she'd been on her first date with Peter more than fifty years ago. Finally, she suggested they all go to the lobby and wait for him there.

The swoosh of automatic doors opening caught their attention. A distinguished, physically fit, white-haired man entered, carrying an armful of red camellias and a gold box. Mom restrained an urge to run into his arms.

"Peter," she said. She thought her heart might beat out of her chest.

He hugged her and kissed her on the lips. A little too long. Mom said she thought Vennetta gasped.

Quick introductions were made.

"Ladies, welcome to Atlanta," Peter said. He presented the flowers to Vennetta and the gold box to Margaret. She raised an eyebrow.

"Homemade candy in honor of your visit," Peter said.

Margaret opened the box and popped a goody in her mouth. "Delicious!"

Peter suggested a cold drink, and the women followed his lead and to a booth in the bar. Mom watched him order and initiate conversation. She had forgotten how sociable he was. "It was as rewarding as watching a favorite movie from the past," she told me later.

"Are you retired now, Peter?" Margaret asked.

"Yes, I am," he answered. "But I have a different idea about retirement than most people. I love to tend my garden, and experiment with new recipes, and I work as an Amway dealer in my spare time so I don't get bored."

"Do you have a brother?" Margaret joked.

Peter talked nonstop—filling in the ladies on his college degree in business, his retired status of colonel, and the house he built in Sandy Springs. Mom was as impressed as Vennetta and Margaret at all he had accomplished over the years.

"Oh my, why am I doing all the talking?" Peter finally said, like someone coming up for air.

The women eyed each other. "Because you're nervous?" Margaret guessed.

Peter's face reddened and he smiled at Mom. "Guilty."

When Vennetta suggested a nap Margaret frowned . . . but then nodded like she finally got it.

Peter and Mom walked around the hotel grounds. He held her hand briefly. Mom loved being alone with him again, but it felt a little awkward.

"Can I make lunch for all of you tomorrow?" Peter asked.

Mom nodded. She was curious about the house he had described—the one he had built with Vivian.

When Mom returned to the hotel room, she found her pals laughing and watching television. They erupted with questions about Peter. Mom answered until they ran out of steam and curiosity. She took the opportunity to jab them about their so-called nap.

The next day, Mom and her pals followed Peter's directions to his house in Sandy Springs. She pulled into the driveway, partially hidden by mature dogwood, oak, and pine trees along with flowering azaleas. The drive meandered across a bridge before the house came into full view atop a knoll. It was an understated, off-white Frank Lloyd Wright style house with a low roofline and extended eaves flanked by lush magnolia trees. A brick walkway lined with cascading flower pots led the way to the front door. Mom followed the drive to its end behind the house. As the women climbed out of the car, they couldn't help notice a plentiful garden with left-over evidence of tomato plants and wandering vines.

"Oh no," Vennetta said. "I'll bet he cans and freezes, just like you did on the farm."

"And look over there," Margaret pointed to a small tractor. "I thought he was a city boy."

Peter opened the back door adjacent to the generous deck. "Ladies, I heard you drive in and was waiting at the front door. What are y'all looking at?"

Mom explained that they were flabbergasted by the size of the garden. She asked if he had a surplus every year.

"Not really," Peter said. "I freeze what I don't need."

The women broke into gales of laughter, which confused him. He figured out it must be an inside joke and let it go.

The immaculate house was decorated with traditional furniture, accented by Asian collectibles and antiques. Soft music played in the background. The cherry dining room table was set with crystal stemware, sterling silver, and fine china, and enhanced with a centerpiece of camellias.

"Wow," Margaret said. "What are we having?"

"First some chilled white wine and smoked salmon dip followed by a healthy vegetable lunch . . . butter beans, creamed corn, and green beans with homemade corn bread and for dessert, apple cake," Peter said as he filled their glasses.

Vennetta sipped her wine. "Fabulous! Did you make this too?" Peter smiled as she continued. "I'd love a tour."

Peter led the women through the house. Mom tried to focus her attention on the décor, but found herself searching each room for signs of the past. Vivian, to be specific, but she saw none.

The women showered praise on the design of the house and the extensive landscaping of the three-acre property. When Peter suggested a tour of his workshop, the ladies finally lost interest and returned to the dining room. Lunch was tasty and not too filling. At least until the apple cake.

"I need a wheelbarrow to get myself back to the hotel," Vennetta exclaimed. "Everything was so scrumptious. You are a gracious host, Peter."

When Peter suggested cooking for all of them again the next night, Vennetta reluctantly said that she and Margaret had plans to meet up with some Ohio friends. Margaret eventually nodded agreement.

"How about you, darling?" Peter said to Mom.

She flushed. "I, uh . . . yes. I'd love to come."

The well-fed ladies piled into their car after lengthy good-byes. No one spoke until they got out onto the road, as if there were hidden bugs to detect their conversation.

"Are you nervous about being alone with him, Elise?" Vennetta asked.

Mom thought for a moment. "No, I don't think so, but ask me again tomorrow."

Margaret poked Mom from the backseat. "Good for you, Elise, for being honest. I'd be shaking in my boots."

The next evening, Mom waited in the lobby of Terrace Gardens. She considered going back to the room for water because her throat felt suddenly dry. She discovered a breath mint in the bottom of her purse. Sucking on it calmed her. She glanced around the lobby at the comings and goings of several well-dressed couples and tried to invent situations for why they were staying there, a game she had started with Sally and me years earlier.

She told me later that remembering some of my more outlandish scenarios made her grin and relax a bit.

Peter pulled up in front of the lobby and waved. She hurried to meet him before he even made it out of the car. He made a joke about her impatience.

"It's true. I hate to wait," she conceded.

He reached across the seat for her hand and told her he thought they'd go back to his house for a cocktail before their dinner reservations.

"You're not cooking for me?" she said.

He looked away before he answered. "We're going to an old favorite of mine—Canoe on the Chattahoochee River. I wanted to give you my undivided attention."

It took an hour to drink one glass of wine. Mom and Peter talked like a couple of long-lost pals. They cried. They laughed. They kissed.

"Oh, my goodness, Lise. It's eight o'clock. I need to get you to that dinner I promised."

Mom didn't want to leave. She suggested they set up a picnic style dinner with assorted crackers and a jar of peanut butter. They sat in front of the living room fireplace, where a blazing fire kept them warm.

"I'm so glad you came to Atlanta, even though the time is going by way too fast," he said pausing for a moment. "Do you think we could visit again? Just you and me?" Mom nodded.

"Tell us everything," Margaret said like an excited teenage girl. "Unless of course you don't want to."

Mom scowled and disappeared into the bathroom.

Margaret motioned to Vennetta and mouthed, "What did I say?"

Several minutes later, Mom emerged in pajamas with red eyes and a runny nose. She fluffed up the pillows against the headboard and plopped down. Vennetta and Margaret waited for her to talk.

"I still feel the same way about him, no matter what I told him back then," Mom said. "And he should hate me after what I did to him . . . I misled and hurt him so."

That November 1994 trip included a couple of visits with Kitty in her retirement home, which abounded with heavily bejeweled old ladies. But it was hard to focus on much other than the reunion with Peter.

"Peter's phone calls and presence kept us buzzing. I thought about him all the time but I tired of all the interrogations and 'what if' questions from Vennetta and Margaret," she admitted to me later.

"Did Kitty make any comment about you seeing Peter?" I asked.

Mom said Kitty knew of the visits and phone calls but never commented on her circumstances.

"And you never asked her what she thought?" I said.

Mom said she was probably too afraid to hear the answer, even though she conceded that Kitty probably wouldn't have expressed anything negative.

The night before the women left, Peter had a chance to be alone with Mom one last time. He held her hand and told her that seeing her had been bittersweet—he didn't want her to leave.

"Maybe you could come to Ohio," Mom suggested.

"Of course. Why not? I would go anywhere to visit you. When are you thinking?"

They discussed the possibilities and decided on the Christmas holidays. Peter said that he wanted to stay a while when he came to Ohio. Mom beamed.

"How long is a while? Two weeks?" she guessed.

He grinned as big as a kid who just won a teddy bear at the county fair. "At least two weeks. Maybe longer."

She nodded and leaned over to kiss him. He held her there like he may never let her go.

Two weeks before Christmas, Vennetta, Margaret, Alta, and Mom made their annual trek to downtown Cleveland for lunch and their gift exchange. They loved to wander through Higbee's, stopping on various floors to look but not buy. They "oohed" and "awed" over the decorations and winter fashions. The mission was lunch, gossip, and buying each other gag gifts.

"I think I'll just have soup," Mom said, once the ladies had been seated for lunch.

Margaret asked Mom how much weight she had lost since their Atlanta trip. Mom shrugged.

"You have lost weight, though, haven't you? You look like you're about a size eight now," Margaret prodded.

"I guess," Mom admitted, "I just feel good in my skin."

After they exchanged their gifts, Mom posed a question for the table. "Do y'all think I'm too old to shop at Victoria's Secret?"

Everyone laughed, everyone except Mom. "I'm serious," she said.

Margaret spoke up. "Well, I guess that depends on what you're shopping for. What'd you have in mind?"

Peter called every day. Sometimes Mom called him a second time. I didn't know then how often they were talking, but I did know they were staying in contact and that Peter had planned a trip to Ohio. I clearly heard the change in Mom's tone of voice when we spoke on the phone; it could have lifted the spirits of the most downtrodden. I told her that I thought her metabolism must be in overdrive with all of her giddy enthusiasm.

"Were you ever a cheerleader?" I teased.

She rattled off several activities that she planned for Peter's visit.

"Ma, do you really think he wants to do all that stuff? I mean, I think he's coming to see *you*."

She stopped midstream. "We like the same things," she said.

I gave up. We vowed to talk again before the big reunion.

Mom said she woke up early the day before Peter arrived. She decided to take a brisk walk to Medina High School. She was so full of anticipation. The night before Peter had shocked her with his parting words on the phone, "Cant wait to see you, we do have some unfinished business."

She was fairly certain she knew what he meant, but was surprised it was still on his mind. They were both seventy-five years old, after all. She phoned me and shakily relayed the conversation.

"Do you think he meant what I think he meant?" she asked me. I paused a second, trying to decide how to ask the delicate question.

"Mom, did you ever have sex with him?" I said.

"No. Of course not."

"Then that's what he's talking about," I said.

"That's what I thought, too, but I wanted a second opinion," she admitted. Mom told me she couldn't remember the last time she had sex, which I told her was more information than I needed.

"We're so old. I mean, I had no idea it would still be such a priority," she said.

I laughed. Then I laughed some more and wished her luck.

Peter had told her to meet him at baggage claim but Mom arrived at the airport two hours before his plane landed. She wanted to surprise him at the gate. She said she never read *The Cleveland Plain Dealer* more thoroughly than that morning.

Mom daydreamed until she heard a voice on the PA system announce, "Flight 55 from Atlanta arriving at Gate 9."

She stood up quickly, as if she might miss it and hurried to find a slot close to the door. She waited for what seemed like an eternity. Peter wasn't the first person to deplane, but almost. He jogged down the jetway and waved to Mom, who looked right at him and grinned.

"Three weeks is too long to be apart," he said and hugged her. He kissed her like a twenty-year-old home on leave. It embarrassed Mom a little, but she didn't pull away.

A few passengers snickered and worked their way around the couple.

"So this is Cleveland?" Peter said as the two walked hand-in-hand toward baggage claim. "Kind of gray and cloudy, but then again, I didn't come for the weather or the scenery."

Mom pointed out various landmarks on the drive back to Medina. Peter nodded politely, but he was distracted.

"Is something wrong?" she said.

He said that nothing was wrong since he was finally with her. "How much longer until we get to your place?"

Once they got to the condo, Mom lit candles and put on music. She had trouble containing her nervous laughter. They talked for a while and she gave him a tour, during which he complimented her decorating skill. Finally, they sat on the couch and kissed for a bit until Peter got up and led her to bed for their first time.

Mom relayed what happened next in a phone conversation we had sometime after Christmas. Actually, I finally asked her directly, and she shyly admitted that yes, they had slept together.

"But you're not married!" I kidded.

"Peter said waiting fifty-five years was long enough," she said.

I laughed, but she didn't seem finished with reliving the event.

"We were both so nervous. Like a couple of teenagers. It would have been very funny if it hadn't been so wonderful," she said. "Afterward, we had the best two-hour nap in history."

With the anguish of their long-time desire for each other satisfied, the pair went on a whirlwind of socialization: meeting Rich, dancing, hosting dinners with Mom and Harlan's old neighbors, enjoying television, and preparing meals together. They had fifty-five years of catching up to do and the two weeks ended in the blink of an eye.

Peter packed his suitcase the day before Christmas as Mom watched. She refolded one of his dress shirts.

"I feel like I saw six movies back-to-back every day. Fun but intense, not to mention exhausting," he said.

Mom asked him if he really needed to go home. She didn't want to be without him on Christmas. Peter didn't need much encouragement—he phoned Delta Airlines and made the flight change.

Both were so elated to have three extra days that they celebrated by going out to dinner. Peter poured champagne and offered a toast. "Here's to you, Elise."

They clinked glasses.

Mom smiled. "And here's to you for forgiving me."

Peter gazed into her eyes. "When we get married, do you think you'll want to live in my house? Or should we buy something together?"

"When we get married? You haven't asked me yet," Mom said.

Peter pushed his chair out, got down on one knee, and looked up at her. He took her hand and kissed it.

"Elise, will you marry me?" he asked.

"Yes."

Several patrons stared at them. Mom realized it must have looked bizarre, given their age, but she was too happy to be shy about causing a scene.

"Oh, the ring. Let's see what I've got," Peter said as he pulled a small box out of his jacket pocket and opened it.

Mom burst into tears. "It's my same ring! After all these years, you kept it?"

He slipped it on her finger. It fit as perfectly and felt as good as when she was twenty-one.

"I couldn't get rid of it. Just couldn't do it. Maybe I knew somehow that this day would happen," Peter said.

Three days later, Mom drove Peter to the airport. She hadn't slept well and had woken up on edge. Introducing Peter to some of the old neighbors hadn't gone well—she'd overheard remarks like "kind of soon" or "wonder just how long they've been talking?" Mom's old habit of worrying what people thought about her was a hard one to kick.

When she confessed her uneasiness to Peter, he told her not to worry over that sort of thing. "Harlan was sick for two years. You and I know we kept our vows to our spouses. That's all that matters."

Mom called me after Peter left. She rattled on about all the activities: lunch at Pier W on Lake Erie, water aerobics, dancing at the old ballroom in Olmstead Falls, roller-skating with Vennetta, and dinner at The Oaks on Chippewa Lake. Listening to the agenda made me tired and after several minutes I interrupted.

"When are you getting married?" I said.

The line went silent for several seconds. "After the first of the year, but no one knows that yet."

"Uh-huh. I'm happy for you, Mom," I said. "I really am."

The line went silent again. For a minute I thought I'd lost the connection, seldom was she at a loss for words.

She sighed. "I'll be moving to Georgia of course. That could be upsetting to Rich and Sally."

I assured her that it wouldn't be a problem once they learned of the impending marriage, they would figure out a move was inevitable. When she said she'd already told them and they seemed happy for her I added, "See? I told you it'd be okay."

*   *   *

Vennetta and Margaret dropped in shortly after Peter's visit and suggested a bus trip to New York City for New Year's Eve. They raved about the package deal that included transportation, hotel, and tickets to Radio City Music Hall with a gala party afterward.

"Just the three of us?" Mom asked. She worried about Alta being left out, as the three of them seemed to be doing more things together.

"We invited Alta, but she said no," Vennetta explained.

Mom jumped on the opportunity to do one last thing with her pals. It would be an excellent send-off before moving to Georgia.

"I'd love to go. And I have some news," Mom said. "Peter and I are getting married."

Margaret's mouth dropped open. Vennetta shook her head and sat down.

"Oh no, Elise. At your age?" Vennetta's neck flushed.

Mom was stunned by their objection. "But we want to make a commitment. It had been our plan so long ago, and now we have the opportunity to do it. There is still time. We know that we want to be together, for as long as possible, as husband and wife. We simply do not believe in that living together arrangement."

No one spoke. Mom said it was awful. Margaret finally picked up her purse and started to head for the door.

"How soon is this going to happen?" she asked.

"In two months or so," Mom said.

When they boarded the bus to New York the next day, Vennetta sat down beside Mom, with Margaret in front of them. They talked about teaching—how they missed it and how glad they were to be done with it. They talked about their kids and Ohio. They talked about everything *except* Peter and the upcoming major change in Elise's life.

After the first rest stop, Margaret switched seats with Vennetta. The bus hadn't even pulled back onto the turnpike before she started in.

"Elise, this is not the right thing to do, this marriage to Pete," she said firmly as she locked eyes with Mom. Margaret waved her index finger like a parent would do to a wayward child.

The bus lurched as the driver accelerated in order to merge into traffic.

"I'm sorry you feel that way," Elise said.

But Margaret was relentless and proceeded to list all the reasons why the marriage to Peter was a bad idea: Mom was too old; she'd probably end up burying yet another husband; she'd be moving back home, which never works out; she'd lose her freedom to do whatever she wanted, and she should consider what family and friends would think of her since Harlan had only been dead two months. Vennetta leaned around the seat and nodded in a way that suggested she agreed with Margaret.

As Margaret's rant continued, Mom's initial anger wilted into hurt feelings. She decided to just let Margaret wind down. Maybe her friends were jealous, or maybe they didn't want to lose a friend.

"I love him, Margaret. There's so little time left . . . can't I do what I want with the rest of my life?" Mom asserted. By then, tears streamed down her cheeks.

Margaret stopped. She reached over and squeezed Mom's hand. "Are you sure, absolutely sure?"

Mom dried her eyes and turned to face Margaret. "I've never been more sure of anything in my whole life."

Margaret nodded and left Mom to sit with Vennetta for the rest of the trip. Several hours later, the threesome marched off the bus into the hotel. Mom held back as the two of them chatted and walked together. When they got to registration, Margaret let Vennetta go ahead and waited.

"I'm sorry, Elise. Very sorry to have hurt your feelings. I only want the best for you," Margaret said.

Mom smiled at her friend and thanked her, feeling the tension already beginning to evaporate.

"Wow, you are quick to forgive," I said later when Mom phoned to tell me about the trip. "I would have decked her."

Mom laughed.

"So how'd the trip go? It must have strained everything," I said.

"Oh no, we actually had a great time. In hindsight, I was glad their disapproval came out in the open where we could deal with it. We'd been through a lot together. And I'm sure it was impossible for them to understand my feelings for Peter. Neither of them had ever had a deep love."

"Did you tell Peter what happened?" I asked. "It might have colored his opinion of them."

"When I got back to Ohio, I phoned him. By then I wasn't mad or hurt. Their actions didn't upset him after all. He said you just had to give people time and they'd come around."

Her capacity for forgiveness amazed me. I realized I still had a lot to learn from her in that regard.

*   *   *

Mom and Peter decided to get married in Sarasota. They wanted warm weather so everyone could have a sunny vacation after the ceremony. Peter's good friend, a retired minister, was in Florida at that time and agreed to perform the ceremony.

Within weeks Mom and Peter arranged their wedding and reception. Forty or so guests witnessed the short service, including Rich, Sally, me, Vennetta, Margaret, Alta, Margaret, several Atlanta friends, and other relatives. Kitty wasn't able to attend which disappointed Mom.

Elise and Peter held hands during their vows and cried as they exchanged their promises to each other.

I cried, quite unexpectedly. Sally told me later that although she was happy for Mom, it seemed like she'd lost her.

Her remark stunned me. She sensed it and explained further.

"I mean that she is on to her new life . . . with Peter in Georgia. Her focus will be that—not us, not grandchildren," Sally said.

I thought about it for a while and eventually understood. She might be right but Mom had given us fifty years of her life and I decided that was enough. Mom and Peter radiated happiness. No doubt that was the key to looking younger.

The reception was held at a garden club, which had a lovely indoor/outdoor venue and was complete with a sumptuous dinner and dancing. Peter welcomed everyone.

"Thank you all for coming. There were times when I thought this day would never happen. Never could happen. But sometimes you just hold onto the dream. My dream of fifty-five years came true today. Before I ask my bride to honor me with the first dance to what will surely become our theme song, I'd like to propose a toast."

The bandleader gave a drum roll.

Peter raised his champagne glass. "To my Elise—she's always been *my* Elise. We had the sunrise, now we'll have the sunset . . . we just missed the day."

Tommy Dorsey's "At Last" filled the room, and the two danced as if they had been dancing together for years—their movement in sync as one as they glided across the floor.

Edwards Brothers,Inc!
Thorofare, NJ 08086
11 January, 2011
BA2011011